GARDEN GUIDE
FOR AUSTIN & VICINITY

FIFTH EDITION, SPRING 2015

COPYRIGHT ©2000-2015 BY THE TRAVIS COUNTY
MASTER GARDENERS ASSOCIATION

**Winner of Texas Master Gardener Association
First Place Award for Exemplary Achievement in Publications,
Years 2000 and 2010**

TEXAS A&M
AGRILIFE
EXTENSION

PUBLISHED BY
THE TRAVIS COUNTY MASTER GARDENERS ASSOCIATION

GARDEN GUIDE
FOR AUSTIN & VICINITY

FIFTH EDITION, SPRING 2015

Published by The Travis County Master Gardeners Association, Inc., an educational, nonprofit, service corporation which renders sound, non-biased horticultural information to the community. Our objectives are accomplished through the volunteer efforts of association members.

Disclaimer: The information herein is for educational purposes only. References to commercial products or trade names are made with the understanding that no discrimination is intended and no endorsement by the Travis County Master Gardeners Association, Inc. is implied.

For more information please check out our website: www.tcmastergardeners.org or call our Master Gardeners Help Desk, 512-854-9600 Monday-Friday, 8am-5pm. You can also email your gardening questions to us at: travismg@ag.tamu.edu

Printed on Recycled Paper

Fifth Edition, Spring 2015
ISBN 978-0-615-30738-1

**Original Designer and Former Editor
Dolores Svoboda Leeper**

**Garden Guide Cover Art © 2015
Designed by Cheryl Harrison**

Printed by Republic Print & Mail
8905 McCann Dr.
Austin, Texas 78757
512-459-4139

For ordering information, please visit the Publication section of our website: www.tcmastergardeners.org

WELCOME TO GARDENING IN AUSTIN & VICINITY

ACKNOWLEDGMENTS/THANKS/DEDICATION

Welcome to the fifth edition of the Garden Guide for Austin & Vicinity. For many of us, gardening is an integral part of not just our homes, but our lives. In fact, President Thomas Jefferson expressed how many of us feel about our gardens when he said, "No occupation is so delightful to me as the culture of the earth, and no culture comparable to that of the garden." It is my hope that this guide will help local gardeners in creating a delightful culture of their own right here in central Texas.

Originally, this project started as an idea to create a garden calendar and evolved into the gardening guide. Gardening in central Texas is not always as easy as planting a seed, adding water, sitting back and enjoying our success. We have hot and dry summers, rocky hillsides, and heavy clay soils among our challenges. Learning from our triumphs and mistakes of what to plant where and when becomes essential to overcoming those challenges.

Featured in the Garden Guide for Austin & Vicinity, Fifth Edition, are:

- Monthly guides to help direct your landscaping and gardening efforts at the right time for this climate.
- Recommended varieties of vegetables, flowers, trees, shrubs and more for this area.
- Resources to call upon, including local organizations, nurseries, suggested reading, web resources and local gardening clubs.
- An introduction to some of the best programs for landscape water conservation and pest control.

In this edition, information has been updated and expanded including the important numbers section, local farmer's market list, plant lists, local nurseries, suggested readings, and web resources. On many pages additional information has been added to many pages as well for further research, including websites, book titles or local club to contacts.

The bulk of the information contained in the Garden Guide for Austin & Vicinity, Fifth Edition, was gathered from two main resources, Skip Richter former Travis County Horticulture Agent, the incredible website at Texas A&M University, and the Central Texas Horticulture website. Additional input and help came from a number of Travis County Master Gardeners.

I would also like to give a special thanks to the following for their help with this fifth edition: Cheryl Harrison for her tireless work inputting edits, Patty Leander, Jean Love El Harim, Sue Colbert and Marc Opperman (Republic Print & Mail) for the amazing photographs used on the front cover and throughout the document. Thanks to all who helped with previous editions: Liz Caskey and Frankie Hart. Thanks to Travis County Texas A&M AgriLife Extension Horticulture Agent, Daphne Richards for her continued support of this project. This fifth edition is dedicated to the incredible Dolores Leeper, Travis County Master Gardener, former editor of and the driving force behind the original creation of this publication. Without her vision and determination, the Garden Guide for Austin & Vicinity would not have become a reality. Thank you, Dolores for your outstanding contributions to the gardening education of the gardeners of Travis County and beyond.

Joe Posern, President Travis County Master Gardeners Association, a service arm of Texas A&M AgriLife Extension, Travis County

GARDENING IN CENTRAL TEXAS

"Whether you're a life-long resident of Central Texas or a recent transplant, you should know that you live in one of the most wonderful places in the nation for gardening." That was how I introduced the fourth edition of this guide, published in 2009, and I still believe it today. Although we sometimes have more than our fair share of Texas-sized challenges, more often than not we have a gardening situation that residents in the rest of the nation would kill for. Our south-central geographic location provides us with many qualities of both the east and the west, as well as the normally mild and pleasant climate of the south. Our warm autumn nights, mild winters and spring rainfall create a spectacular gardening climate for three seasons of the year. Unlike most of the nation, summer is by far the harshest season for us. Most years, summer forces itself upon us (complete with brutual temperatures, intensely sunlight, and drought) before spring even gets a chance to say hello, leaving our landscapes and gardens hurting and in need of attention by the time autumnal relief arrives.

More challenging than summer heat for some Central Texas gardeners is learning how to live with their soil. To the east are the blackland prairies and fertile river bottom soils of the Colorado River, where heavy clay may be a problem. And to the west are the limestone outcroppings where soil is thin and rocky (or perhaps virtually non-existent), and the pH is very high. These climatic and topographical challenges can be frustrating to newcomers, as well as to those who have been gardening in the Austin area for many years. But with the knowledge of just a few gardening basics specific to Central Texas, you can be successful in your efforts. Site preparation, careful plant selection, and efficient irrigation design can make a big difference.

Since our fourth edition was published seven years ago, Central Texas has gone through some pretty brutal climatic extremes, including 2011, when we chalked up a record 90 official days of 100+ degree temperatures and weathered one of the most severe droughts in history. That same year, raging wildfires consumed entire communities just to our north and east; and just a few years later, at the opposite extreme, record rainfall and flooding events not only wiped out gardens, but also decimated entire neighborhoods. Getting through these times has been tough, not only for home gardeners and their landscapes, but also for farmers, nurserymen and green industry professionals. The climatic extremes have also taken a toll on our community greenbelts and other natural areas. Times like these remind us that we have to work in harmony with our environment to increase our chances for success.

With our population exploding, natural resources are in greater demand than ever. Even in years with ample rainfall, water conservation will continue to be a huge issue here in Central Texas, across the entire state, and in the rest of the nation. With irrigation restrictions in place, we may only be able to give our plants just enough water to survive the harsh heat and drought of summer, so they've to be water-thrifty and resilient, as well as beautiful and tasty. Many people are moving away from large, expansive lawns and embracing low-water-use native plants in their landscapes. These plants give our area an attractive look with the flair that is unique to Central Texas, and they offer the climate and soil tolerance often lacking in non-native species. There is a rugged beauty to our area that can and should be used as an asset in our landscaping styles.

Whether you're looking to spruce up and maintain the landscape you have, install new areas and make big changes for water conservation, or grow more of your own food, our goal is to help you be successful in your gardening efforts. This guide is packed with specific, local information and resources, and I know you'll find it useful as you navigate through the seasons and challengest that are unique to our beautiful community.

From Augie and I; best wishes for a beautiful, productive, water-conserving, joy-inducing, Central Texas garden.

Daphne Richards

Daphne Richards, County Extension Agent – Horticulture
Texas A&M AgriLife Extension Service, Travis County

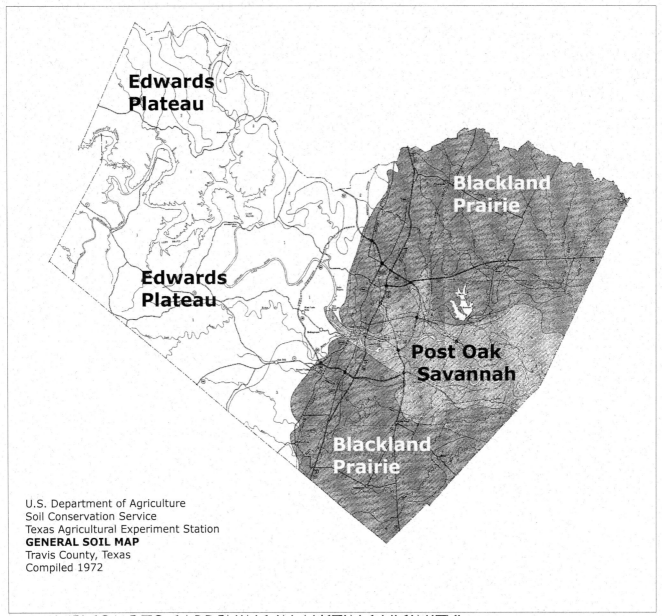

Edwards Plateau

Edwards Plateau

Blackland Prairie

Post Oak Savannah

Blackland Prairie

U.S. Department of Agriculture
Soil Conservation Service
Texas Agricultural Experiment Station
GENERAL SOIL MAP
Travis County, Texas
Compiled 1972

WELCOME TO GARDENING IN AUSTIN & VICINITY!

Some facts and figures:

- Altitude ranges from 400 to 1300 feet above sea level (average is 630 feet within Austin);
- Rainfall averages 33.78 inches per year; (less in the Hill Country);
- Growing season (days without frost or freezes) averages 270 days;
- Average last spring freeze is March 3; (latest on record - April 9);
- Average first fall freeze is November 28; (Earliest on record - October 24);
- USDA Hardiness Zone 8b (average lowest temperature is 15 to 20 degrees); and
- AHS Heat Zone 9 (number of days per year temperature is above 86 degrees ranges from 120 to 150).

Austin is unique, that's why you live here or got here just as fast as you could. But so are Austin's soils—and not knowing your soil and the plants that will grow and thrive on your lot could be costly both in time and money. The Central Texas region consists of several soil and climate combinations which means that landscape decisions should be specific to your site.

Three distinct vegetation areas meet in Austin: *the Edwards Plateau, the Blackland Prairie, and the Post Oak Savannah*. Each of these areas has different soil types with different planting requirements. The native and adaptive (non-native plants that do well in this climate) plants that will thrive on these soils are also very different. Before you plant, take this tour of Austin soil types and choose your landscape to fit.

The Edwards Plateau is generally west of Mopac. This area features shallow soils with rolling hills and steep slopes. West Lake Hills, Oak Hill, and Rollingwood are representative communities. Commonly referred to as the beginning of the Texas Hill Country, the Plateau's undeveloped areas are dominated by mesquites, oaks, and cedars (really junipers). When you choose a homesite in the Hill Country, take stock of the existing vegetation and develop a plan with your builder to protect it during construction. Avoid indiscriminate clearing of the land in this very ecologically-sensitive area. Limit fill only to that required to ensure adequate drainage away from the foundation. Avoid cheap "sandy loam" fill. It is usually an infertile product referred to by landscapers as "red death." Use a "landscapers mix" instead.

The majority of new plants in the landscape should be native or adapted to the area. For trees, select bur and chinquapin oaks, cedar elm, Chinese pistache, Mexican buckeye, Mexican plum, Texas persimmon and Texas redbud. For shrubs, select Texas mountain laurel, yuccas, native bunch grasses or yaupon holly.

The Blackland Prairie is generally east of the Balcones Fault. Soils in this area are mainly deep and the terrain is gently sloping. Sunset Valley and Manchaca are right on the dividing line. The intersection of the Missouri Pacific and Southern Pacific rails (Mopac) at McNeil Drive is just west of the line. Undeveloped homesites in this area were once farmland. Fertile areas near Del Valle and Govalle were used as truck gardens at the turn of the century and provided early Austinites with fresh produce. Existing vegetation may include grasses and scrub brush. Existing trees may consist of oaks, pecans, and some cedars. Pecans and oaks are excellent selections for new landscapes. Some shrub choices include cherry laurel, Indian hawthorn, oleander, and Burford,

Chinese, or yaupon holly.

The Post Oak Savannah is generally east of Austin. Indicators for this area are sandy, slightly acidic soil with post oaks. Some references include this area in the Blackland Prairie or in a more inclusive area referred to as the Cross Plains and Timbers, so plants from Blackland Prairie lists may be appropriate for your specific site. Some landscape plans for this area may include some of the selections from both the Blackland Prairie and the Edwards Plateau lists. This may seem a bit confusing, but look at your actual site. A city-by-city list of regions is included in the "must have" book, *Native Texas Plants - Landscaping Region by Region*, by Sally and Andy Wasowski. Sally suggests starting "with the city you live in or live closest to. Next read about the possible choices for your area. Then go outside, look at your soil, and match it as best you can to one of those described for your area."

Each homesite should be evaluated for the dominant soil type, not by its location on a map. The above regions and soil types are general. Your site may be slightly different from your neighbors', both in soil and climate. If you are unsure about the type of soil, consider getting a soil analysis. This is a free service at some area nurseries, or contact your Travis County Agrilife Extension at 512-854-9600.

Create zones in your landscape according to existing or improved soils. Group plants that have similar soil and water needs together. Keep high water use plants to a minimum and group these together to make a miniature oasis. These small distinct areas can be easily maintained if they are near the front or back door. Be aware of microclimates that exist even on your own property. Author Scott Ogden writes in *Gardening Success with Difficult Soils*, "Even the smallest gardens offer a series of microclimates around the house or grounds that favor various plants and enable a wider variety to be grown." For example, reflected heat from walls or patios can create pockets of warmer temperatures for more tender plants, while plants exposed to cold north winds need to tolerate colder winter temperatures.

Native and adaptive plants thrive the best and are low maintenance. Low maintenance alternatives to traditional landscaping are becoming the norm. In Central Texas, with our hot, dry summers, native and adaptive plants require very little water to thrive. It is not a style of gardening, but a method of gardening.

Source: Residential & Multifamily Programs, Landscape, City of Austin's Green Builder Program

An adequate supply of high quality water has become a critical issue for the future prosperity of Texas. Booming populations have increased the demand on the state's already limited supply of high quality water. In addition, seasonal fluctuations in rainfall and periodic droughts have created a feast-to-famine cycle in Texas.

In urban areas of Texas between 40 and 60 percent of the water supply is used for landscape and garden watering. Much of this water is used to maintain traditionally high water-demanding landscapes, or it is simply applied inefficiently.

In an attempt to reduce the excessive water use, the Texas Agrilife Extension is conducting programs for Texans on Xeriscape landscaping, quality landscaping that conserves water and protects the environment. This concept is an innovative, comprehensive approach to landscaping for water conservation. Traditional landscapes may incorporate one or two principles of water conservation, but they do not utilize the entire concept to reduce landscape water use effectively.

Xeriscape landscaping incorporates seven basic principles that save water:

1. Planning and design
2. Soil analysis
3. Practical turf areas
4. Appropriate plant selection
5. Efficient irrigation
6. Use of mulches
7. Appropriate maintenance

By incorporating these seven principles, you can help conserve our most precious natural resource—water.

Xeriscape landscapes need not be cactus and rock gardens. They can be green, cool landscapes full of beautiful plants maintained with water-efficient practices. The same green Texas-style landscape to which we are accustomed can be achieved and still conserve water.

Start With a Plan

Creating a water-efficient landscape begins with a well-thought-out landscape design. Sketch your yard with existing structures, trees, shrubs and grass areas. Then consider the landscape budget, appearance, function, maintenance and water requirements. Local landscape architects, designers, nurserymen and county extension agents can help in this decision making. Implementing your landscape design can be done gradually over several years.

Soil Analysis and Preparation

Increase plant health and conserve water by adding organic matter to the soil of shrub and flower bed areas. This increases the soil's ability to absorb and store water in a form available to the plant. As a general rule, till in 4 inches of organic material such as shredded pine bark, peat or compost. For areas with trees and grass, however, incorporating organic matter is not economically feasible or necessary.

Plant Selection

Select trees, shrubs and groundcovers based on their adaptability to your region's soil and climate. Texas is blessed with an abundance of beautiful native plants which are naturally adapted to the region. Most require less additional water, less additional fertilizer and have fewer pest problems.

Through the support of the nursery industry, native Texas plants are becoming more available in retail nurseries and garden centers. Combining Texas natives with well-adapted exotic plants is a key to a beautiful, interesting landscape that conserves water. Refer to the tables in this publication and check with your local nursery or county extension agent for recommendations on adapted landscape plants for your area.

Grass Selection

 When considering a landscape's water requirement, it is important to note that turf grasses require more frequent watering and maintenance than most other landscape plants. Carefully select grass according to its intended use, planting location and maintenance requirements.

St. Augustine and Bermuda grasses are most often used for lawns in Texas. Zoysia and new native grass mixes, such as Habiturf®, are used less often but offer much promise for landscape water conservation.

Grasses available for use in Texas lawns vary significantly in water requirements. Planting the lowest water use turf grass adapted to the region is an effective way to reduce landscape irrigation requirements.

Achieve a significant reduction in water consumption and landscape maintenance by reducing the size of water-sensitive lawns. Replace with patios, decks, shrubs, and groundcovers.

Also, when designing or evaluating turf areas in the landscape, consider the ease or difficulty in watering the proposed area. Long, narrow areas and small oddly-shaped areas are difficult for any irrigation equipment to efficiently water. Eliminate long, narrow areas and create more blocky, square areas.

Landscape Maintenance

An added benefit of Xeriscape landscapes is less maintenance. A well-designed landscape can decrease maintenance by as much as 50 percent through reduced mowing; once-a-year mulching; elimination of weak, unadapted plants; and more efficient watering techniques.

Watering

A tremendous amount of water is applied to lawns and gardens. Much of it is never absorbed by the plants and put to use. Some water is applied too rapidly and is lost to runoff. Some water evaporates from exposed, unmulched soil. The greatest waste of water is applying too much, too often.

In addition to overwatering the plant, excess irrigation can leach nutrients deep into the soil away from plant roots and increase the chances of polluting groundwater. Similarly, runoff caused by excess irrigation can carry polluting fertilizers and pesticides to streams and lakes. The waste or pollution of high quality water through inefficient irrigation practices can be eliminated through proper watering techniques.

Lawns

Most lawns receive twice as much water as they require for a healthy appearance. The key to watering lawns is to apply the water infrequently, yet thoroughly. This creates a deep, well-rooted lawn that efficiently uses water stored in the soil. (Note: soil should be a minimum depth of 6 inches.)

Learn when to water the lawn by simply observing the grass. Wilting and discoloration are signs of water stress. At the first sign of wilting, you have 24 to 48 hours to water before serious injury occurs. Apply 1 inch of water to the lawn as rapidly as possible without runoff.

Watering only when needed and then watering thoroughly produces a deep-rooted lawn that is more water efficient and drought enduring.

Trees and Shrubs

All trees and shrubs need more frequent watering from the time of planting until they become well rooted. This may take two growing seasons. Once established, plants can then be weaned to tolerate less frequent watering. Proper weaning develops deep roots and makes the plants more drought enduring.

As with lawns, water established trees, shrubs and groundcovers infrequently, yet thoroughly. In the absence of rain, most trees and shrubs benefit from a once-a-month thorough watering during the growing season. Remember, normal lawn watering is not a substitute for thorough tree and shrub watering.

The feeding root system of a tree or shrub is located within the top 12 inches of the soil and at the "dripline" of the plant. The dripline is the area directly below the outermost reaches of the branches. Apply water and fertilizer just inside and a little beyond the dripline, not at the trunk. Simply lay a slowly-running hose on the ground and move it around the dripline as each area becomes saturated to a depth of 8 to 10 inches. For large trees, this watering technique may take several hours.

Irrigation Systems

The goal of any irrigation system is to give plants a sufficient amount of water without waste. By zoning an irrigation system, grass areas can be watered separately and more frequently than groundcovers, shrubs and trees. Both sprinkler and drip irrigation can be incorporated to achieve water conservation in the landscape.

Sprinkler Irrigation

Sprinkler irrigation is the most commonly used method of landscape watering. The two most common types of sprinkler irrigation systems are the hose-end sprinkler and the permanent underground system. Even though a permanent sprinkler system can be more water efficient than a hose-end sprinkler, both systems require little maintenance and apply large volumes of water in a short time.

If you have a permanent sprinkler system, make sure the sprinkler heads are adjusted properly to avoid watering sidewalks and driveways. Also, a properly adjusted sprinkler head sprays large droplets of water instead of a fog of fine mist which is more susceptible to evaporation and wind drift.

With either hose-end sprinklers or permanent systems, water between late evening and mid-morning to avoid excessive waste through evaporation.

Drip Irrigation

Drip irrigation offers increased watering efficiency and plant performance when compared to sprinkler irrigation. In areas of the state with poor water quality (e.g., high salt content), drip irrigation also allows safer use of "salty water" in the landscape and garden.

Drip irrigation slowly applies water to soil.

The water flows under low pressure through emitters, bubblers or spray heads placed at each plant. Water applied by drip irrigation has little chance of waste through evaporation or runoff.

The best ways to learn more about the many benefits of drip irrigation are to seek professional irrigation advice and to experiment with available drip irrigation products in small sections of the landscape.

Mulching Conserves Moisture

Mulch is a layer of nonliving material covering the soil surface around plants. Mulches can be organic materials such as leaves, pine bark, compost and woodchips; or inorganic materials, such as lava rock, limestone or permeable plastic (not sheet plastic).

Use a mulch wherever possible. A good mulch conserves water by reducing moisture evaporation from the soil. Mulch also reduces weed populations, prevents soil compaction and keeps soil temperatures more moderate.

Proper Mowing Conserves Water

Mowing grass at the proper height conserves water. Mow St. Augustine and buffalo grass  to 3 inches; for Bermuda grass mow to 1 inch; for centipede grass and Zoysia mow to 2 inches. Mowing at these relatively tall heights allows the grass to develop a deeper, more water-efficient root system. Taller grass blades also act as a living mulch, shading the ground and reducing soil moisture evaporation. Finally, as the grass grows taller, it grows slower and matures, and requires less water and mowing.

Proper Fertilizing Conserves Water

Applying fertilizer to the lawn at the right time and in the proper amount can save time, effort and money through reduced mowing and watering. Fertilizers also can be a major source of pollution of streams and groundwater if excessive amounts are applied.

Fertilize the lawn once in the spring and again in the fall to produce a beautiful turf without excess growth which demands frequent watering. Use a slow-release form of nitrogen in the spring application and a quick-release form in the fall. Apply only 1/2 pound of actual nitrogen per 1,000 square feet of lawn at one time. By using this fertilizer schedule, no other fertilizer is needed for most shrubs and trees in the lawn area.

Other Cultural Practices To Save Water

Other cultural practices that add to the efficient use of water by plants are periodic checks of the irrigation system, properly timed insect and disease control and elimination of water-demanding weeds.

Sources: A & M Website:
http://aggie-horticulture.tamu.edu/extension/xeriscape/xeriscape.html

Douglas F. Welsh, Extension Horticulturist, William C. Welch, Extension Landscape Horticulturist
Richard L. Duble, Extension Turf Grass Specialist (retired), Texas Agrilife Extension

WATER CONSERVATION INFORMATION/WATER WISE LANDSCAPING INFORMATION

City of Austin Water Conservation Office
625 E. 10th St., Ste. 615, Austin, TX 78701
512-974-2199 Email: www.austintexas.gov/email/watercon Overview of Educational Programs: www.austintexas.gov/department/water-conservation

Grow Green aims to educate Austin area residents on the least toxic approach to pest management and responsible fertilizer use in order to reduce the amount of landscape chemicals that "run-off" into our waterways and degrade our water quality. Call 512-974-2581 (City of Austin Watershed Protection) for more information. www.austintexas.gov/department/grow-green

Smartscapes is landscaping that emphasizes a simpler approach that allows you to achieve a successful landscape, based on climate, topography, soil type, and life-style. Xeriscapes save money and resources. www.txsmartscape.com

Travis County Agrilife Extension
Daphne Richards, Travis County Horticulturist
1600-B Smith Road, Austin, TX 78721 512-854-9600
http://aggie-horticulture.tamu.edu/travis/

Earth-Kind
Earth-Kind Landscaping uses research-proven techniques to provide maximum garden and landscape enjoyment while preserving and protecting the environment. http://aggie-horticulture.tamu.edu/earthkind/publications/

Lady Bird Johnson Wildflower Center
4801 La Crosse Ave., Austin, TX 78739
512-232-0100 www.wildflower.org

Zilker Botanical Garden
2220 Barton Springs Road, Austin, TX 78746
512-477-8672 www.zilkergarden.org

What is a rain garden? It's a depression in the landscape created to collect and store rainfall until it can infiltrate the soil. Think of them as basins designed to catch and retain stormwater on your property rather than having it rush off to the nearest drain, carrying with it valuable soil and nutrients. They are not the same as bog or water gardens.

Why are rain gardens important?
- delay and reduce stormwater runoff
- increase the amount of water that soaks into the soil
- recharge local and regional aquifers
- reduce local and regional flooding and drainage problems
- protect local waterways from pollutants carried by urban stormwater such as fertilizers and pesticides
- enhance the beauty of your landscape
- provide habitat for birds, butterflies and beneficial insects

Where do you put them?
- at least 10 feet away from any building foundation to prevent structural damage
- in a relatively flat section of your yard
- where water will infiltrate the soil within 24 hours
- in full sun where possible
- never directly over a septic system

What shape and size should it be?
- shape is not a critical factor, but they are often oval or kidney shape with largest side facing the source of runoff in order to maximize capture
- usually twice as long as they are wide
- see references for sizing guidelines, but don't be put off by the math – anything helps!

What maintenance is required?
- remove weeds completely the first two years
- water if needed until plants are established
- prune back each spring to height of 6 to 8 inches
- mulch for the first two years

What plants should you use (see page 13 for a list of suggested plants)?
- choose deep rooted native plants
- purchase plants with well established root systems, at least 1 year old
- design for beauty and color in every season
- the most successful plants are those that tolerate brief periods of standing water and long periods of little or no rainfall - plants for sides and floors of rain gardens will usually have different water requirements

What about mosquitoes?
There won't be any. Remember, rain gardens should be located where the water completely soaks into the soil within 24 hours. Mosquitoes need 7 to 12 days to lay and hatch eggs. Plus, rain gardens attract dragonflies that love to eat mosquitoes.

Okay, now what? Get more detailed information from these references:

"Rainwater Harvesting: Raingardens", AgriLife Extension publication EL-5482, available for free download at http://AgriLifebookstore.org/product-p/el-5482.htm

City of Austin website for information on rain gardens: www.austintexas.gov/department/rain-gardens-keeping-water-land

OUTSTANDING NATIVE & ADAPTED LANDSCAPE PLANTS

GARDENING 'CENTRAL TEXAS STYLE' uses native plants as the starting point to create a guide to earthwise plant selections. A coalition of The Watershed Protection Development Review (City of Austin), The Texas Agrilife Extension, The Grow Green Program has developed a plant list to help select native and adapted plants that are naturally drought tolerant and resistant to pests and diseases. Their free guide **Native and Adapted Landscape Plants** is available through the Travis County Agrilife Extension Office and many area nurseries and includes extensive information about the recommended plants. The **interactive plant database** is also available online at: http://austintexas.gov/department/grow-green/plant-guide

BIG TREES

Texas Ash	*Fraxinus texensis*
Cedar, Eastern Red	*Juniperus virginiana* var. *virginiana*
Cherry, Black	*Prunus serotina* var. *exima*
Cypress, Arizona	*Cupressus arizonica*
Cypress, Bald	*Taxodium distichum*
Cypress, Montezuma	*Taxodium mucronatum*
Elm, Cedar	*Ulmus crassifolia*
Honey Mesquite	*Prosopis glandulosa* var. *glandulosa*
Maple, Big Tooth	*Acer grandidentatum*
Oak, Bur	*Quercus macrocarpa*
Oak, Chinquapin	*Quercus muhlenbergii*
Oak, Lacey	*Quercus laceyi*
Oak, Mexican White	*Quercus polymorpha*
Oak, Southern Live	*Quercus virginiana*
Oak, Texas Red	*Quercus texana*
Palmetto, Texas Palm, or Texas Sabal	*Sabal texana* or *Sabal mexicana*
Pecan	*Carya illinoiensis*
Sycamore, Mexican	*Platanus mexicana*

SMALL TREES/LARGE SHRUBS

Anacacho Orchid Tree	*Bauhinia lunariodes*
Anacua (Sandpaper Tree)	*Ehretia anacua*
Arrow Sweetwood	*Myrospernum sousanum*
Buckeye, Mexican	*Ungnadia speciosa*
Buckeye, Red	*Aesculus pavia* var. *pavia*
Carolina Buckthorn	*Frangula caroliniana*
Cherry Laurel	*Prunus caroliniana*
Crape Myrtle	*Lagerstroemia indica*
Desert Willow	*Chilopsis linearis*
Eve's Necklace	*Styphnolobium affine*
Goldenball Leadtree	*Leucaena retusa*
Holly, Possumhaw	*Ilex decidua*
Holly, Yaupon	*Ilex vomitoria*
Huisach	*Acacia farnesiana*
Kidneywood	*Eysenhardtia texana*
Mountain Laurel, Texas	*Sophora secundiflora*
Olive, Mexican	*Cordia boissieri*
Persimmon, Texas	*Diospyros texana*
Palm, Windmill	*Trachycarpus fortunei*
Plum, Mexican	*Prunus mexicana*
Pomegranate	*Punica granatum*
Redbud, Mexican	*Cercis canadensis* 'mexicana'
Redbud, Texas	*Cercis canadensis* 'texensis'
Retama	*Parkinsonia aculeata*

Roughleaaf Dogwood	*Cornus drummondii*
Silktassel, Mexican	*Garrya ovata* spp. *lindheimeri*
Sumac, Flameleaf	*Rhus lanceolata*
Sumac, Evergreen	*Rhus virens*
Viburnum, Rusty Blackhaw	*Viburnum rufidulum*
Viburnum, Sandankwa	*Viburnum suspensum*
Walnut, Little	*Juglans microcarpa*
Wax Myrtle	*Morella cerifera*
Xylosma	*Xylosma congestum*

SHRUBS

Abelia, Glossy	*Abelia x grandiflora*
Agarita	*Berberis trifoliata*
Apache Plume	*Fallogia paradoxa*
American Beautyberry	*Callicarpa americana*
Aralia, Japanese	*Fatsia japonica*
Baptisia, Purple (Wild Indigo)	*Baptisia australis*
Barbados Cherry	*Malpighia glabra*
Bottlebrush	*Callistemon citrinus*
Butterfly Bush, Wooly	*Buddleja marrubiifolia*
Coralberry	*Symphoricarpos orbiculatus*
Cotoneaster	*Cotoneaster spp.*
Dalea, Black	*Dalea frutescens*
Desert Broom	*Baccaris sarothroides*
Elbow Bush	*Forestirera pubescens*
Flame Acanthus	*Anisacanthus quadrifidus* var. *wrightii*
Fragrant Mimosa	*Mimosa borealis*
Germander, Bush	*Teucrium fruticans*
Greek Myrtle	*Myrtus communis*
Hawthorne, Indian	*Rhaphiolepis indica*
Holly, Dwarf Burford	*Ilex cornuta* 'Burfordii'
Holly, Dwarf Yaupon	*Ilex vomitoria* 'Nana'
Holly, Nellie R. Stevens	*Ilex cornuta* 'Nellie R. Stevens'
Japanese Yew	*Podocarpus macrophllus*
Mallow, Globe	*Sphaeralcea ambigua*
Mistflower, White	*Ageratina havanensis*
Mock Orange	*Philadelphus coronarius*
Palmetto, Texas Dwarf	*Sabal minor*
Pineapple Guava	*Feijoa sellowiana*
Pittosporum	*Pittosporum tobira*
Rose, 'Belinda's Dream'	*Rosa* 'Belinda's Dream'
Rose, 'Cecile Brunner'	*Rosa* 'Cecile Brunner'
Rose, 'Grandma's Yellow'	*Rosa* 'Grandma's Yellow'
Rose, 'Knock Out'	*Rosa* 'Knock Out'
Rose, 'Livin' Easy'	*Rosa* 'Livin' Easy'
Rose, 'Marie Daly'	*Rosa* 'Marie Daly'
Rose, 'Marie Pavie'	*Rosa* 'Marie Pavie'
Rose, 'Martha Gonzales'	*Rosa* 'Martha Gonzales'
Rose, 'Mutabilis'	*Rosa* 'Mutabilis'
Rose, 'Nearly Wild'	*Rosa* 'Nearly Wild'
Rose, 'Old Blush'	*Rosa* 'Old Blush'
Rosemary, Upright	*Rosmarinus officinalis*
Sage, Texas	*Leucophyllum frutescens*
Senna, Flowering	*Cassia corymbosa*
Sweet Almond Verbena	*Aloysia virgata*
Skyflower, Duranta	*Duranta erecta*
Sumac, Fragrant (Aromatic)	*Rhus aromatica*
Thryallis, Golden Showers	*Galphimia glauca*
Turk's Cap	*Malvaviscus arboreus* var. 'Drummondii'

PERENNIALS

Artemesia	Artemesia 'Powis Castle'
Beebalm	Monarda fistulosa
Bird of Paradise, Red	Caesalpinia pulcherrima
Bird of Paradise, Yellow	Caesalpinia gilliesii
Black-eyed Susan,	Rudbeckia hirta var. pulcher rima
Bulbine	Bulbine frutescens
Butterfly Weed, Mexican (Tropical Milkweed)	Asclepias currasavica
Calylophus(Square Bud Primrose)	Calylophus berlandieri
Cast Iron Plant	Aspidistra elatior
Catmint	Nepeta x faassenii
Chile Pequin	Capsicum annuum
Columbine, Red	Aquilegia canadensis
Columbine	Aquilegia chrysantha var. 'Hinkleyana'
Coralbean	Erythrina herbacia
Coreopsis, Lance-leaf	Coreopsis lanceolata
Cuphea, Batface	Cuphea llavea
Cuphea, 'David Verity'	Cuphea 'David Verity'
Daisy, Blackfoot	Melampodium leucanthum
Daisy, Chocolate	Berlandiera lyrata
Daisy, Copper Canyon	Tagetes lemmonii
Daisy, Engelmann	Engelmannia peristenia
Damianita	Chrysactina mexicana
Datura (Jimson Weed)	Datura wrightii
Esperanza/Yellow Bells	Tecoma stans
Fall Aster	Aster oblongifolium
Fern, Firecracker	Russelia equisetiformis
Fern, River	Thelypteris kunthii
Firebush	Hamelia patens
Frostweed	Verbesina virginica
Gaura	Gaura lindheimeri
Gayfeather	Liatris mucronata
Germander, Green	Teucrium chamaedrys
Gregg Mistflower	Conoclinium greggii
Hibiscus, Perennial	Hibiscus spp.
Honeysuckle, Mexican	Justicia spicigera
Hymenoxys (Four Nerve Daisy)	Tetraneuris scaposa
Indigo Spires	Salvia 'Indigo Spires'
Iris, Bicolor	Dietes bicolor
Lamb's Ear	Stachys byzantina
Lantana (hybrid)	Lantana x hybrida
Lantana, Texas	Lantana urticoides
Lantana, Trailing	Lantana montevidensis
Lion's Tail	Leonotis leonurus
Marigold, Mexican Mint	Tagetes lucida
Maximillian Sunflower	Helianthus maximilliani
Obediant Plant, Fall	Physostegia virginiana
Oregano, Mexican	Poliomintha longiflora
Penstemon, Gulf Coast	Penstemon tenuis
Penstemon, Hill Country	Penstemon triflorus
Penstemon, Rock	Penstemon baccharifolius
Phlox, Garden	Phlox paniculata
Plumbago	Plumbago auriculata
Primrose, Missouri	Oenothera macrocarpa
Purple Coneflower	Echinacea purpurea
Rock Rose	Pavonia lasiopetala
Ruellia, Dwarf	Ruellia brittoniana
Sage, Cedar	Salvia roemeriana
Sage, Cherry	Salvia greggii
Sage, Jerusalem	Phlomis fruticosa
Sage, Majestic	Salvia guaranitica
Sage, Mealy Blue	Salvia farinacea
Sage, Mexican Bush	Salvia leucantha
Sage, Penstemon	Salvia penstemonoides
Sage, Russian	Perovaskia atriciplifolia
Sage, San Luis	Salvia microphylla
Sage, Tropical	Salvia coccinea
Senna, Lindheimer	Senna lindheimeriana
Shrimp Plant	Justicia brandegeana
Skeletonleaf Goldeneye	Viguiera stenoloba
Skullcap, Pink	Scutellaria suffrutescens
Skullcap, Heartleaf	Scutelleria ovata subsp. brac teata
Skullcap, Wright's Purple	Scutellaria wrightii
Society Garlic	Tulbaghia violacea
Spiderwort	Tradescantia spp.
Texas Betony	Stachys coccinea
Winecup, Perennial	Callirhoe involucrata
Yarrow	Achillea spp.
Zexmenia	Wedelia texana

YUCCAS/AGAVES/SUCCULENTS/CACTI/SOTOLS

Agave spp.	Agave spp.
Basket Grass (Sacahuista)	Nolina texana
Cactus, Prickly Pear	Opuntia spp.
Nolina	Nolina lindheimeriana
Sotol, Texas	Dasylirion texanum
Yucca spp.	Yucca spp.

ORNAMENTAL GRASSES

Bluestem, Little	Schizachyrium scoparium
Indiangrass	Sorghastrum nutans
Inland Seaoats	Chasmanthium latifolium
Muhly, Bamboo	Muhlenbergia dumosa
Muhly, Big	Muhlenbergia lindheimeri
Muhly, Deer	Muhlenbergia rigens
Muhly, Gulf	Muhlenbergia capillaris
Muhly, Pine	Muhlenbergia dubia
Sedge, Meadow	Carex perdentata
Sideoats Grama	Bouteloua curtipendula
Switchgrass	Panicum virgatum

VINES

Alamo Vine	Merremia dissecta
Carolina Jessamine	Gelsemium sempervirens
Crossvine	Bignonia capreolata
Fig Vine	Ficus pumila
Honeysuckle, Coral	Lonicera sempervirens
Jasmine, Star	Trachelospermum jasminoides
Mexican Flame Vine	Pseudogynoxys chenopodioides
Passion Vine	Passiflora incarnata
Rose, Lady Banksia	Rosa banksiae
Trumpet Vine	Campsis radicans
Virginia Creeper	Parthenocissus quinquefolia
Wisteria, Texas	Wistera frutescens

GROUNDCOVERS

Aztec Grass	Ophiopogon intermedius
Clover Fern	Marsilea macropoda
Dalea, Gregg	Dalea greggii
Frogfruit	Phyla nodiflora
Germander, Creeping	Teucrium cossonii
Golden Groundsel (Roundleaf Ragwort)	Packera obovata
Horseherb	Calyptocarpus vialis
Iceplant	Aptenia spp.; Delosperma spp.; Malephora spp.
Leadwort Plumbago	Ceratostigma plumbaginoides
Liriope	Liriope muscari
Monkey Grass (Mondo Grass)	Ophiopogon japonicus
Mountain Pea	Orbexilum pedunculatum
Oregano	Origanum vulgare
Pigeonberry	Rivina humilis
Purple Heart	Secreasea pallida
Santolina (Lavender Cotton)	Santolina chamaecyparissus
Sedges	Carex spp.
Sedum (Stonecrop)	Sedum spp.
Silver Ponyfoot	Dichondra argentea
Snakeherb	Dyschorisste linearis
Verbena	Verbena spp.
Violet	Viola missourensis
Wavy Scally Cloak Fern	Astrolepis sinuate
Wooly Stemodia	Stemodia lanata

WATER PLANTS

American water willow	Justicia americana
Arrowhead	Syngonium podophyllum
Bandana-of-the-Everglades	Canna flaccida
Cardinal flower	Lobelia cardinalis
Coastal water-hyssop	Bacopa monnieri
Delta arrowhead	Sagittaria platyphylla
Giant bulrush	Seripus acutus
Horsetail	Equisetum arvense
Jamaican sawgrass	Cladium mariscus spp.
Lance-leaf burhead	Echinodorus tenettus
Lizard tail	Saururus cernuus
Long-leaf/knotty pondweed	Potamogeton nodosus
Marsh fleabane	Pluchea odorata
Marsh obedient plant	Physostegia intermedia
Pickerelweed	Pontederia cordata
Powdery thalia	Thalia dealbata
Salt marsh-mallow	Kosteletzkya virginica
Scarlet rose-mallow	Hibiscus coccineus
Soft rush	Juncus effusus
Spider-lily	Amaryllidaceae
Trisquare bulrush	Syngonium podophyllum
Virginia blueflag	Iris virginica
Water clover	Marsilea mutica
White water lily	Nymphaea odorata
White-topped sedge/star sedge	Dichromena colorata
Wooly rose-mallow	Hibiscus lasiocarpus

Yellow cow-lily/Spatterdock	Nuphar polysepala
Yellow water lotus	Nelumbo lutea
Zig-zag iris	Iris brericaulis

BULBS

Amaryllis
Bearded Iris
Chinese Ground Orchid
Daffodils
Lilies, Cooper's
Lilies, Crinum
Lilies, Oxblood/Schoolhouse
Lilies, Spider
Oxalis (can be aggressive, do not plant near preserves)
Rainlilies

RAINGARDEN

Base of the garden:

Bushy Bluestem	Andropogon glomeratus
Cardinal Flower	Lobelia cardinalis
Eastern Gamagrass	Tripsacum dactyloides
Fall Obedient Plant	Physostegia virginiana
Frogfruit	Phyla nodiflora
Gregg's Mistflower	Conoclinium greggii
Horsetail	Equisetum arvense
Inland Sea Oats	Chasmanthium latifolium
Marsh Obedient Plant	Physestegia intermedia
Maximilian Sunflower	Helianthus maximilliani
Salt Marsh Mallow	Kosteletzkya virginica
Scarlet Rose Mallow	Hibiscus coccineus
Slender Rush	Juncus tenuis
Soft Rush	Juncus effusus
Swamp Milkweed	Asclepias incarnata
Swamp sunflower	Helianthus angustifolius
Switchgrass	Panicum virgatum
Water Clover	Marsilea mutica
White-topped Sedge	Dichromena colorata
Wooly Rose-Mallow	Hibiscus coccineus

Sides of the garden:

Big Bluestem	Andropogan gerardii
Big Muhly	Muhlengergia lindheimeri
Black-eyed Susan	Budbeckia hirth
Brazos Penstemon	Penstemon tenuis
Clasping Coneflower	Rudbeckia amplexicaulis
Cut-leaf Daisy	Engelmannia pinnatifida
Deer Muhly	Muhlengergia rigens
Eastern Gamagrass	Tripsacum dactyloides
Gulf Coast Muhly	Muhlenbergia capillaris
Illinois Bundleflower	Desmanthus illinoesis
Marsh Fleabane	Pluchea odorata
Pink Evening Primrose	Oenothera speciosa
Pitcher Sage	Salvia azurea
Plains Coreopsis	Coreopsis tinctoria
Prairie Wildrye	Elymus canadensis
Scarlet Sage	Salvia coccinea

Material from **Native and Adapted Landscape Plants,** an Earthwise Guide for Central Texas. Published by the City of Austin, Travis County Agrilife Extension and Grow Green.

TEXAS SUPERSTAR™ PLANTS

Plants designated as "TEXAS SUPERSTARS" are hardy, tolerating the hot dry summers characteristic of most parts of the State. They are disease and insect tolerant, providing beauty with minimal care and minimal reliance on chemical pest control.

www.texassuperstar.com

Annuals:
Angelonia Serena™ Series
Baby's Breath Eurphorbias
Texas Bluebonnets
Texas Maroon Bluebonnets
Lady Bird Johnson Royal Blue Bluebonnet
Cool Season Euphorbias
Gophrena, Globe Amaranth
Dakota Gold Helenium
Larkspur
Rio Series Mandevillas
'Mari-mum' (African type marigold)
Laura Bush Petunia Petunia
'Tidal Wave™ Cherry' Petunia
'Tidal Wave™ Silver Petunia
Butterfly Deep Pink Pentas
Vinca Cora Series

Perennials:
Texas Gold Columbine
Flare Hibiscus
Lord Baltimore Hibiscus
Moy Grande Hibiscus
New Gold™ Lantana
Trailing Lantana
Malaviscus, Turk's Cap
Princess Caroline Napier Grass
Dwarf Mexican Petunia
John Fanick Phlox
Victoria Phlox
Plumbago
Mexican Bush Sage
'Henry Duelberg' Salvia
'Mystic Spires Blue' Salvia
'Blue Princess' Verbena

Per-Annuals:

Duranta, Brazilian Sky Flower
Gold Star Esperanza
Firebush
Firecracker Jatropha
Variegated Tapioca
Thryallis

Woody Shrubs:
Lynn's Legacy Cenizo
Belinda's Dream Rose
Grandma's Yellow Rose
Knock Out™ Rose
Marie Daly Rose
Texas Lilac Vitex

Trees:
Deciduous Holly
Shantung Maple
Lacey Oak
Chinkapin Oak
Chinese Pistache

Specialty Plants:
'Natchez' Blackberry

'Green Magic' Broccoli
Graptophyllum, Caricature Plant
Phalaenopsis Orchids
Satsuma Mandarin
'Orange Frost' Satsuma
'NuMex Twilight' Ornamental Pepper
'Dwarf Cherry Surprise', 'BHN 968' Tomato
'Tycoon' Tomato
Waterlilies

ANNUALS BY LANDSCAPE CHARACTERISTICS

Easy-to-Grow
Cosmos, Portulaca, California Poppy, Purple Fountain Grass, Celosia, Marigold, Coleus, Vinca, Petunia, Zinnia
Shade or Semi-shade
Coleus, Salvia, Impatiens, Begonia
Hot, Dry Locations
Cosmos, Narrow Leaf Zinnia, Portulaca, Vinca
Poor Soils
California Poppy, Portulaca, Iceland Poppy, Purple Fountain Grass, Celosia
Hardy and Half-Hardy
Petunia, Phlox, California Poppy, Iceland Poppy, Larkspur, Dianthus, Ornamental Kale, Pansy
Sow or Transplant in Fall
Pansy, Cosmos, California Poppy, Iceland Poppy, Larkspur
May Self-Seed Year after Year
Cosmos, Nicotiana, Pansy, Impatiens, Portulaca, Larkspur, California Poppy, Vinca, Zinnia
Can be Direct-Seeded
Iceland Poppy, California Poppy, Larkspur, Marigold, Gomphrena, Zinnia
Use as Cut Flowers
Salvia, Larkspur, Celosia, Phlox, Cosmos, Zinnia
Suitable for Drying
Gomphrena, Celosia, Strawflower, Statice
Grow for Fragrance
Nicotiana, Phlox, Dianthus, Petunia, Moonflower, Stock
Grow for Colorful Foliage
Dusty Miller, Purple Fountain Grass, Coleus, Ornamental Kale
Use for Edging
Dusty Miller, Petunia, Begonia, Phlox, Portulaca, Coleus, Marigold (dwarf), Zinnia (dwarf), Dianthus, Pansy
Suitable for Containers
Phlox, Impatiens, Portulaca, Begonia, Marigold, Coleus, Pansy, Petunia
Suitable for Backgrounds and Screens
Cosmos, Marigold (tall varieties), Purple Fountain Grass, Celosia (tall varieties), Zinnia (tall varieties)
Suitable for Use as Groundcover
Narrow Leaf Zinnia, Portulaca, Vinca
Attracts Birds
Petunia, Salvia, California Poppy, Portulaca, Zinnia
Attracts Hummingbirds and Butterflies
Phlox, Salvia, Verbena, Narrow Leaf Zinnia

TOP PERENNIALS FOR LANDSCAPE USE

Coreopsis, Daylily, Goldstrum Rudbeckia, Perennial Hibiscus, Purple Coneflower, Garden Canna, Turk's Cap, 'Texas Gold' Columbine, Firebush, Perennial Verbena.

Guideline Codes: A-Annual/P-Perennial/DS-Direct Seed/ T-Transplant/S-Shade/PS-Part Shade/Sun-Full Sun

Plant	Jan	Feb	Mar	Apr	May	Jun	Jul	Aug	Sep	Oct	Nov	Dec	Guidelines*
Alyssum, Sweet	█	█	█							█	█	█	A/DS/PS
Aster, Stokesia			█	█	█	█	█	█	█				P/T/SUN
Balsam, Garden			█	█	█	█	█	█	█				A/DS/SUN/PS
Begonia, Wax				█	█	█	█	█	█				A/P/T/PS
Calendula	█	█	█						█	█	█	█	A/DS/T/SUN
Celosia				█	█	█	█						A/DS/SUN
Centaurea	█	█	█						█	█	█	█	A/DS/SUN
Cleome				█	█	█	█	█	█				A/DS/SUN/PS
Coleus			█	█	█	█	█	█	█				A/T/SUN
Coreopsis			█	█	█	█	█	█	█				P/DS/SUN
Cosmos, Early			█	█	█	█	█	█	█				A/DS/SUN
Dusty Miller		█	█	█	█	█	█	█	█	█			A/T/SUN
Gomphrena				█	█	█	█	█	█				A/DS/SUN
Hamelia				█	█	█	█	█	█				P/T/SUN
Impatiens			█	█	█	█	█	█					A/T/PS
Jacobinia			█	█	█	█	█	█	█				P/T/PS
Lantana			█	█	█	█	█	█					P/T/SUN
Larkspur	█	█							█	█	█	█	A/DS/SUN
Marigold				█	█	█	█	█					A/DS/SUN
Mexican Heather			█	█	█	█	█	█					A/T/SUN
Nasturtium			█	█					█	█			A/DS/PS
Nicotiana				█	█	█	█	█	█				A/T/SUN/PS
Pansies	█	█								█	█		A/T/SUN
Pentas			█	█	█	█	█	█	█				A/T/PS
Periwinkle				█	█	█	█	█					A/T/SUN
Petunia			█	█	█	█	█	█					A/T/SUN/PS
Poppies									█	█			A/DS/SUN
Purslane/Portulaca				█	█	█	█	█					A/T/SUN
Salvia Spp.			█	█	█	█	█	█	█				P/T/SUN
Snapdragon	█									█	█		A/DS/SUN
Sweet Pea										█	█		A/DS/SUN
Verbena			█	█	█	█	█	█					P/A/T/SUN
Johnny-jump-up	█	█								█	█	█	A/DS/T/SUN
Zinnia				█	█	█	█	█					A/DS/SUN

BERRY VARIETIES

Blackberries
Brazos, Kiowa, Rosborough
Blackberries, Thornless
Apache, Arapaho, Natchez
Strawberries
Chandler, Seascape, Sequoia

NUT AND GRAPE VARIETIES

Grapes
Black Spanish (Le Noir), Blanc du Bois, Champanel, Favorite, Lake Emerald, Verdelet, Victoria Red
Pecans
Caddo, Cape Fear, Cheyenne, Choctaw, Desirable, Forkert, Houma, Kiowa, Oconee
Walnuts
Reda, Geoagiu 86, Geoagiu 3 X 4 X 453, Germisara, Orastie

EDIBLE FLOWERS

Borage, calendulas, carnations, chamomile, chives, chrysanthemums, dandelions, daylilies, gardenias, geraniums, gladioli, lavenders, lilies, marjoram, nasturtiums, pansies, peonies, primroses, roses, squash blossoms, sweet violets and yucca blossoms have different edible portions that are nutritious and tasty.

Fresh, whole flowers of gladioli, roses, squash, pansies and lilies are now sold at farmer's markets as edible flowers along with nasturtiums and yucca blossoms. When portions of edible flowers are desired, pull petals or edible portions from fresh flower or snip off the petal from the base of the flower. Remember to always wash flowers thoroughly to make certain all chemical or organic pesticides have been removed. Give them a gentle bath in salt water and then dip the petals in ice water to perk them up. Drain on paper towels. Petals and whole flowers may be stored a short time in plastic bags in refrigeration. Freeze whole small flowers in ice rings or cubes. Web info about **edible flowers**: www.whatscookingamerica. net/EdibleFlowers/EdibleFlowersMain.htm and www.foodsubs.com/Flowers.html.

FRUIT TREE VARIETIES

Apples
Fuji, Granny Smith, Mollie's Delicious, Mutsu, Pink Lady, Smoothee
Citrus-Lemons
Improved Meyer
Citrus-Lime
Mexican Lime
Citrus-Satsuma
Miho, Seto, Owari, Orange Frost
Figs
Alma, Celeste, LSU Purple, Texas Ever bearing/Brown Turkey
Jujubes
Chico, Honey Jar, Li, Lang, Shanxi Li, Sherwood, Sugar Cane, Winter Delight
Peaches-Freestone
Dixiland, Flavorcrest, Gala, Goldprince, Harvester, Hawhtorne, Juneprince, La Felicina, Southern Pearl, Tex Royal, Texstar
Peaches-Cling
Bicentennial, Junegold, Regal
Pears
Ayers, Garber, Kieffer, LeConte, Magness, Moonglow, Orient, Warren, 20th Century
Persimmons-Asian, Non-astringent
Fuyu, Ichikikei Jiro (dwarf), Izu Suruga, Cholate (Astringent when seedless)
Persimmons-Asian, Astringent
Hachiya, Honan Red, Saijo, Tamopan
Plums
Allred, Methley, Robusto, Santa Rosa
Pomegranates
Cloud, Fleischmans, Granada, Wonderful

Call the Travis County Agrilife Extension Office at 512-854-9600 for the Fruit and Nut Tree Spray Schedule.

Fruit Tree Pruning
Fruits develop on last year's growth. Trim new branch growth by about half and long shoots no more than one-third. Remove thin, spindly shoots, as they tend to produce less. Remove low-hanging branches. Thin out the center. Maintain a workable height of 8-12 feet.
Blackberry Cane Pruning
Prune as soon as fruit is harvested. Remove old canes to the ground. Tip new canes when they reach 3-4 feet to encourage branching.

Vegetable Garden Planting Guide

Daphne Richards, County Extension Agent - Horticulture

Texas AgriLife Extension Service, Travis County, 1600-B Smith Road, Austin, TX 78721   512-854-9600

TEXAS A&M
AGRILIFE
EXTENSION

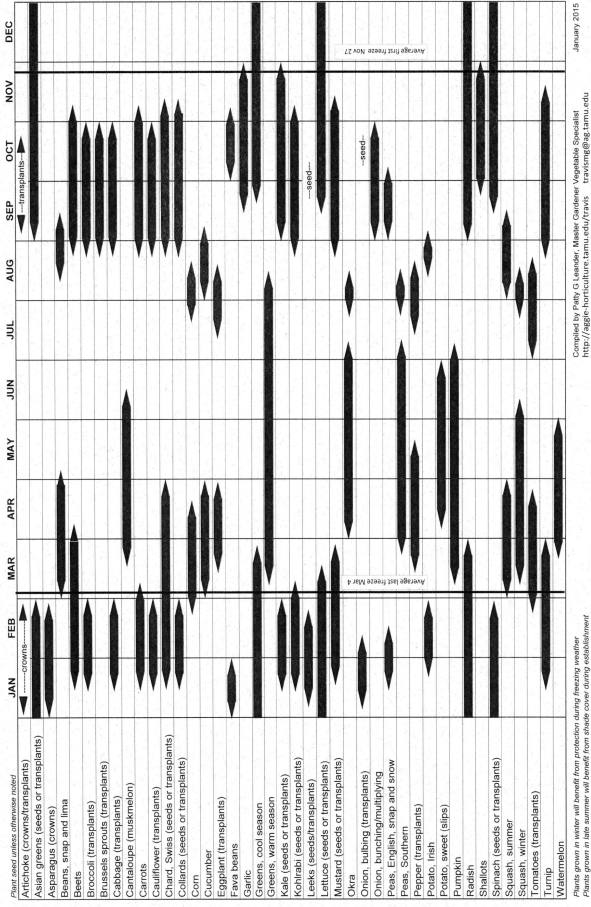

Plant seed unless otherwise noted

Artichoke (crowns/transplants)
Asian greens (seeds or transplants)
Asparagus (crowns)
Beans, snap and lima
Beets
Broccoli (transplants)
Brussels sprouts (transplants)
Cabbage (transplants)
Cantaloupe (muskmelon)
Carrots
Cauliflower (transplants)
Chard, Swiss (seeds or transplants)
Collards (seeds or transplants)
Corn
Cucumber
Eggplant (transplants)
Fava beans
Garlic
Greens, cool season
Greens, warm season
Kale (seeds or transplants)
Kohlrabi (seeds or transplants)
Leeks (seeds/transplants)
Lettuce (seeds or transplants)
Mustard (seeds or transplants)
Okra
Onion, bulbing (transplants)
Onion, bunching/multiplying
Peas, English, snap and snow
Peas, Southern
Pepper (transplants)
Potato, Irish
Potato, sweet (slips)
Pumpkin
Radish
Shallots
Spinach (seeds or transplants)
Squash, summer
Squash, winter
Tomatoes (transplants)
Turnip
Watermelon

JAN   FEB   MAR   APR   MAY   JUN   JUL   AUG   SEP   OCT   NOV   DEC

Average last freeze Mar 4

Average first freeze Nov 27

----crowns----
----transplants----

--seed--
--seed--

Plants grown in winter will benefit from protection during freezing weather
Plants grown in late summer will benefit from shade cover during establishment

Compiled by Patty G Leander, Master Gardener Vegetable Specialist
http://aggie-horticulture.tamu.edu/travis   travismg@ag.tamu.edu

January 2015

RECOMMENDED VEGETABLE VARIETIES

ARTICHOKE: Green Globe, Imperial Star

ASPARAGUS: UC 157, Jersey Giant, Mary Washington

ASIAN GREENS: Joi Choi, Komatsuna, Mei Qing Choi, Mizuna, Tatsoi

BEANS—*Green, Bush:* Contender, Derby, Dwarf Horticulural (pinto), Maxibel, Provider, Roma II

BEANS—*Green, Pole:* Garden of Eden, Kentucky Wonder, Louisiana Purple Pod, McCaslan

BEANS—*Fava:* Broad Windsor

BEANS—*Lima, Bush:* Dixie Butterpea, Fordhook 242, Henderson Bush, Jackson Wonder

BEANS—*Lima, Pole:* Christmas, Florida Speckled, King of the Garden

BEETS: Bull's Blood, Chiogga, Cylindra, Detroit Dark Red, Golden, Red Ace, Ruby Queen

BROCCOLI (transplants): Arcadia, Calabrese, Green Magic, Gypsy, Packman

BRUSSELS SPROUTS (transplants): Churchill, Diablo, Long Island Improved

CABBAGE (transplants): Bilko (Chinese), Early Jersey Wakefield, Famosa (savoy), Fast Vantage, Michihili (Chinese), Red Express, Tendersweet

CANTALOUPE (Muskmelon): Ambrosia, Hale's Best

CARROTS: Chantenay Red Core, Danvers 126, Mokum, Nelson, Scarlet Nantes

CAULIFLOWER: Cheddar (orange), Graffiti (purple), Snow Crown, Snowball Y, Veronica (green)

CELERY: Tango, Utah 52-70

CHARD—*Swiss:* Bright Lights, Fordhook, Rhubarb Red

COLLARDS: Champion, Georgia Southern

CORN: Ambrosia (se), Country Gentleman (OP), Kandy Korn (se), Luscious (se), Silver Queen (su)

CUCUMBER—*Pickling:* Calypso, Carolina, Eureka, Homemade Pickles

CUCUMBER—*Slicing:* Diva, General Lee, Salad Bush, Straight Eight, Suyo Long, Sweet Slice, Tasty Green

EGGPLANT (transplants): Black Beauty, Nadia, Ping Tung Long, Rosa Bianca

GARLIC: California Early, Creole Red, Lorz Italian

GREENS—*Specialty (Cool Season):* Arugula, Corn Salad/Mache, Radicchio Red Preco

GREENS—*Specialty (Warm Season):* Lambsquarter, Malabar Spinach, Molokhia, New Zealand Spinach, Vegetable Amaranth

KALE: Dwarf Blue Curled, Red Russian, Scarlet, Toscano (Dino Kale), Winterbor

KOHLRABI: Early Purple Vienna, Early White Vienna, Kolibri

LEEKS (transplants): American Flag, King Richard, Lancelot

LETTUCE—*Leaf & Bibb:* Black Seeded Simpson, Buttercrunch, Lollo Rossa, New Red Fire, Salad Bowl

LETTUCE—*Romaine:* Jerico, Parris Isalnd Cos, Rouge d'Hiver, Winter Density

MUSTARD: Osaka Purple, Red Giant, Southern Giant

OKRA: Burgundy, Clemson Spineless, Emerald, Hill Country Red, Stewart's Zeebest

ONION—*Bulbing (transplants):* 1015Y TX Supersweet, Candy, Southern Belle (Red), White Bermuda, Yellow Granex

ONION—Green/*Bunching:* Evergreen White, Multiplier

PEAS—*English:* Little Marvel, Wando

PEAS—*Snap:* Cascadia, Sugar Ann, Super Sugar Snap

PEAS—*Snow:* Dwarf Grey Sugar, Oregon Sugar Pod

PEAS—*Southern*: California Blackeye #5, Mississippi Silver, Pinkeye Purple Hull, Zipper Cream

PEAS—*Yard Long/Asparagus Bean:* Liana, Red Noodle

PEPPER—*Hot (transplants):* Anaheim, Cayenne-Long Red, Habanero, Hungarian Wax, Poblano, Serrano, Tabasco

PEPPER—*Jalapeño (transplants):* Garden Salsa, Mucho Nacho, TAM Mild

PEPPER—*Sweet (transplants):* Big Bertha, Blushing Beauty, California Wonder, Carmen, Cubanelle, Gypsy, Marconi, Pimento L, Sweet Banana

POTATOES—*Irish:* Kennebec (white), Red La Soda, Red Pontiac, Yukon Gold

POTATOES—*Fingerling:* Austrian Crescent, Russian Banana

POTATOES—*Sweet:* Beauregard, Centennial, Georgia Jet

PUMPKIN: Connecticut Field, Jack-B-Little, Orange Smoothie, Small Sugar

RADISH: Champion, Easter Egg, French Breakfast, Chinese Red Meat, White Icicle

RADISH—*Daikon:* Miyashige, Summer Cross

SPINACH: Bloomsdale (savoy), Space (smooth), Tyee (semi-savoy)

SQUASH—*Summer (Patty Pan):* Benning's Green Tint, Sunburst, White Bush Scallop

SQUASH—*Summer (Yellow):* Butterstick, Dixie Crookneck, Multipik, Zephyr

SQUASH—*Summer (Zucchini):* Black Beauty, Costata Romanesco, Eight Ball, Raven, Tatume

SQUASH—*Winter:* Bon Bon Buttercup, Small Wonder Spaghetti, Sunshine Kabocha, Table Queen Acorn, Waltham Butternut

SQUASH—*Winter (Specialty):* Carnival, Delicata, Sweet Dumpling

TOMATOES*—*Cherry (transplants):* Black Cherry (I), Juliet (I), Sun Gold (I), Sweet Baby Girl (I), Sweet 100 (I), Yellow Pear (I)

TOMATOES*—*Paste (transplants):* Roma (D), Viva Italia (D)

TOMATOES*—*Standard (transplants):* Big Beef (I), Black Crim (I), Celebrity (Semi-det), Cherokee Purple (I), Early Girl (I), Juane flammé (I), Tycoon (D), Stupice (I)

TURNIPS: Hakurei, Purple Top White Globe, Seven Top (greens only), Tokyo Cross

WATERMELON: Black Diamond, Crimson Sweet, Jubilee, Mickylee, Moon and Stars, Sugar Baby

*D=Determinate, I=Indeterminate

Updated and revised by Daphne Richards, Travis County Extension Agent, Horticulture, and compiled by Patty Leander, Master Gardener, January 2015.

Plan your garden so that the same vegetables of the same family group are not planted in the same area every season.

Family groups are:
1. **Composite**
   lettuce, chicory, endive, escarole, salsify, dandelion, Jerusalem artichoke
2. **Goosefoot**
   Swiss chard, beets, spinach
3. **Grass**
   corn, sweet corn
4. **Legumes**
   peas and beans of all types
5. **Lily**
   onions, garlic, leek
6. **Mustard**
   cabbage, cauliflower, broccoli, Brussels sprouts, rutabaga, kale, turnip, mustard, radish, collard
7. **Nightshade**
   tomato, potato, eggplant, pepper, tomatillo
8. **Parsley**
   carrot, celery, parsley, parsnips
9. **Squash**
   watermelon, cucumber, squash, cantaloupe, honeydew melon, pumpkin

Select a well-drained garden site to prevent damping-off and other root related problems associated with wet soil.

Watering plants in the evening causes leaves to remain wet for an extended period and increases the chance of leaf diseases. Plants watered early in the morning dry quickly, resulting in fewer problems. Drip irrigation also reduces foliage diseases and saves water.

CREATE A BACKYARD WILDLIFE HABITAT
Landscape with native plants to promote wildlife habitat

Just provide the four necessary elements:
Food-shrubs and trees for fruits, seeds. Perennial and annual flowers for nectar. Supplemental feeders for hummingbirds (nectar) and seeds for songbirds
Water-bird baths, shallow dish on ground
Cover-evergreen trees and shrubs, rocks, brush
Places to raise young-nest boxes, host plants, ponds, a variety of deciduous and evergreen trees and shrubs, annual and perennial flowers.

For more information see the **National Wildlife Federation**: www.nwf.org/ or Texas Park & Wildlife: www.tpwd.state.tx.us/huntwild/wild/wildscapes

Shady and Wet

Blue Boneset
Cast Iron Plant
Cardinal Flower
Crinum
Fern
Ginger
Louisiana Iris
Peruvian Lily
Spider Lily
Turk's Cap
Umbrella Sedge

Shade

Calla Lily
Caladium
Cast Iron Plant
Columbines
Ferns
Gingers
Gold Dust Plant
Guernsey Lily
Hosta
Impatiens
Jacobinia
Persian Shield

Sunny and Wet

Blue Boneset
Cannas
Giant Rose Mallow
Hardy Ageratum
Horsetail
Lythrum
Papyrus
Sagittaria
Salt Marsh Mallow
Spider Lily
Umbrella Sedge
Violet-stemmed Taro

Hot and Dry

Coral Vine
Cockscomb
Daylily
Esperanza
Fire Bush
Guara
Hymenoxys
Lantana
Santolina
Mexican Sage
Red Yucca
Rockrose
Verbena
Zinnia Linearis

VEGETABLE	LIKES	DISLIKES
Asparagus	Tomatoes, parsley, basil	
Beans	Potatoes, carrots, cucumbers, cauliflower, cabbage, summer savory, most other vegetables and herbs	Onions, garlic, gladiolus
Pole Beans	Corn, summer savory	Onions, beets, kohlrabi
Bush Beans	Potatoes, cucumbers, corn, strawberries, celery, summer savory	Onions
Beets	Onions, kohlrabi	Pole beans
Cabbage Family	Aromatic plants, potatoes, dill, celery, chamomile, sage, peppermint, rosemary, beets, onions	Strawberries, tomatoes, pole beans
Carrots	Peas, leaf lettuce, chives, onions, leeks, rosemary, sage, tomatoes	Dill
Chives	Carrots	Peas, beans
Corn	Potatoes, peas, beans, cucumbers, pumpkins, squash	
Cucumbers	Beans, corn, peas, radishes, sunflowers	
Tomatoes	Chives, onion, parsley, asparagus, nasturtium, carrot	Kohlrabi, potatoes, fennel, cabbage
Eggplant	Beans	
Peas	Carrots, turnips, radishes, cucumbers, corn, beans, most vegetables and herbs	Onions, garlic, gladiolus, potatoes
Squash	Nasturtium, corn	
Onions & garlic	Beets, strawberries, tomatoes, lettuce, summer savory, chamomile	Peas, beans
Lettuce	Carrots, radishes, strawberries, cucumbers	
Radish	Peas, nasturtium, lettuce, cucumbers	
Parsley	Tomatoes, asparagus	
Potatoes	Beans, corn, cabbage, horseradish, marigold, eggplant--as lure for Colorado potato beetle	Pumpkins, squash, cucumbers, sunflowers, tomatoes, raspberries
Pumpkins	Corn	Potatoes
Strawberries	Bush beans, spinach, borage, lettuce	Cabbage
Spinach	Strawberries	
Sunflowers	Cucumbers	Potatoes
Turnips	Peas	

The soil soaks up and holds water and nutrients like a sponge. These nutrients are held in liquid solution around the soil particles but are also held by negative charges on the soil particles, much like a magnet holds bits of metal. The nutrients are then slowly released to plants.

Soils differ in nutrient content and ability to hold nutrients. Clay or loam soils, and soils high in organic matter hold much more nutrients than sandy soils. Likewise, nutrients differ in their ability to be "tied up" or held in the soil. Phosphorus tends to "stick around" for years while nitrogen is readily lost.

Plants require at least 16 different nutrients for growth and fruiting. The three nutrients required in largest quantities are nitrogen, phosphorus and potassium. These are the nutrients represented on a fertilizer label. A 15-5-10 fertilizer, for example, contains 15% nitrogen, 5% phosphorus and 10% potassium. Other nutrients are just as important, but are required in much smaller amounts.

Plant nutrition is a complex matter. Nutrients interact with each other in complicated ways so that an imbalance can be as detrimental as a shortage. Fertilizing with the same product year after year, with no consideration of the soil's nutrient content can create problems for plants. Indiscriminate fertilizing can also be harmful to the environment. Misapplied and overapplied fertilizer accounts for a large part of the pollution in our surface and groundwater supplies.

Although general guidelines may be given, fertilizer recommendations cannot be made accurately without a soil test to indicate the levels of nutrients present in the soil.

If you have not taken a soil test in the lawn, garden or orchard in the last three years, do so this year. Sample bags and forms are available at the Travis County Agrilife Extension Office: 512-854-9600. Having your soil tested is a good start toward growing a beautiful landscape or bountiful garden. Soil reports provide basic information on the nutritional condition of the soil. Necessary corrections can then be made to avoid poor plant growth and loss of yield.

Skip Richter
Former Travis County Extension Director

Texas A & M Soil Testing Laboratory:
http://soiltesting.tamu.edu/
Alternative Soil Testing
Laboratories Agronomy Resource List
https://attra.ncat.org/attra-pub/soil_testing/

JANUARY

1	
2	
3	
4	
5	
6	
7	
8	
9	
10	
11	
12	
13	
14	
15	
16	
17	
18	
19	
20	
21	
22	
23	
24	
25	
26	
27	
28	
29	
30	
31	

/garden notes

A GARDENER'S RESOLUTIONS FOR THE NEW YEAR

This year I will:

♦ Buy that top-of-the-line hand tool I have been dreaming of and take good care of it, too.
♦ Plant something for the birds and bees to enjoy. Maybe some sunflowers, salvias, lantana and Turk's cap.
♦ Adopt a native flower, shrub or tree.
♦ Plant an extra row of veggies and donate them to the local food bank.
♦ Grow heirloom varieties along with the new, improved ones. See which does better for me.
♦ Add a fun garden ornament to the landscape—a gazing ball, wind chime.
♦ Feed my soil, not my plants. (Make compost!)
♦ Introduce at least one child to the wonders and joys of gardening.
♦ Read a gardening book and grow some new ideas for my garden.
♦ Start a garden journal so I can remember when that inch of rain really fell.
♦ Wear sun protection and gloves. Drink lots of water and stretch before I start my gardening chores.
♦ Reduce my stress levels and get my exercise and fresh air by weeding and lifting bags of potting soil.
♦ Give thanks for all the miracles of life and growth surrounding me in my garden.
♦ Take time to smell the roses and pet the cats and dogs and watch more sunsets.

Holidays/Observances this month:

New Year's Day, Epiphany, Martin Luther King's Birthday, Benjamin Franklin's Birthday

THINGS TO PLANT IN JANUARY

FLOWER PLANTS: Alyssum, Butterfly Weed, Calendula, Candytuft, Cornflower, Dianthus, Daisy (African, Michaelmas and Painted), Gaillardia, Liatris, Edging Lobelia, Nasturtium, Ornamental Cabbage and Kale, Pansy, Phlox paniculata, Snapdragon, Stock.

FLOWER SEEDS: Ageratum, Alyssum, Balsam, Bluebell, Calendula, Candytuft, Cleome, Coreopsis, Cornflower, Delphinium, Echinacea, Feverfew, Gaillardia, Gayfeather, Gerbera, Hollyhock, Hyacinth, Larkspur, Lobelia, Lupine, Nasturtium, Phlox drummondii, Poppy, Queen Anne's Lace, Petunia, Snapdragon, Sweet Pea, Sweet William.

BULBS: Allium, Alstroemeria, Amarcrinum, Canna, Crinum, Dahlia, Daylily, Gladiolus, Hosta, Hyacinth, Spider Lily (Hymerocallis), Liriope, Monkey Grass, Rain Lily, Society Garlic, Tigridia, Tulip.

VEGETABLES:
Early—Mid Month: Asparagus crowns.
Mid—Late Month: Broccoli, Cabbage, Carrots, Cauliflower, Kohlrabi, Lettuce, Onion transplants, Peas (English & edible pod), Spinach.

HERBS: Garlic Chives, Horseradish, Parsley, Chervil.

FRUIT: Bare root or container grown pecans, fruit trees, grapes and berry bushes.

THINGS TO DO IN JANUARY

FERTILIZE: Fertilize asparagus, strawberries, daylilies, iris, pansies and roses. Use compost, manure or a complete fertilizer.

WATER: Water everything well before a freeze, but avoid overwatering.

TRANSPLANT: Plant bare root and container grown roses, shrubs, trees, groundcovers and vines. Move hardy seedlings outdoors. Divide and transplant perennial herbs and summer and fall blooming perennial flowers. Donate extras to a plant sale.

PREPARE SOIL: Add compost and/or fertilizer. Loosen the soil. Test soil (forms available at the Extension Office). Check winter mulch and replenish, if needed. Stockpile leaves for mulch and composting throughout spring and summer.

LAWN CARE: If lawn has a history of brown patch problems, treat with a labeled fungicide late in the month. Repeat treatment in three to four weeks, if needed.

DISEASES/PESTS TO LOOK FOR: Check for mealy bugs and for scale on houseplants. Need a plant problem identified? Just bring a sample in a ziplock bag to the Travis County Agrilife Extension Office, 1600-B Smith Road.

CALL: The Travis County Agrilife Extension Office 512-854-9600 for fruit and nut tree spray schedules.

OTHER THINGS TO DO

Time to get the garden ready for the new growing season. Clean, repair and replace garden tools. Create a garden plan to help organize chores and planting schedules. Start tomato, pepper and eggplant seedlings indoor under fluorescent lights.

IN PRAISE OF ORGANIC MATTER

The cycle of nature in which plants and animals live, grow, die and return their nutrients to the soil is truly a masterfully designed system. In the process, the soil is mulched to reduce erosion and compaction, and plants are fed via a slow-release source of nutrients as organic matter decomposes.

Gardeners have long known the many benefits of organic matter. They have repeated its accolades as the miracle ingredient for loosening clay soils, improving the holding capacity of sands, fighting weeds as a mulch, buffering pH fluctuations and releasing nutrients. As the Travis County Horticulturist, I've exhorted gardeners to "add compost" countless times as a solution to a variety of ills. Yet despite seeing it work miracles over and over, I still marvel when I see it again. I relearn the lesson of organic matter each time I garden in a new spot. Until the soil is rich with compost and has mellowed for a season or so, the new garden just seems to struggle.

Organic materials like leaves, grass clippings and composted bark contain the nutrients the plant took up during the growing season. In fact they include just the right blend of nitrogen, phosphorus, potassium, magnesium, iron, zinc, etc. that a plant needs. As these organic materials decompose they become a bank account of all these nutrients in the soil.

Composting is the process of speeding up the natural decomposition of organic materials in a rather controlled setup. Whether in a bin or freestanding compost heap, we mix the high carbon materials with high nitrogen materials, wet the mix and then let the natural process speed along. Whether you buy compost or make it yourself, it is "black gold" for the garden! It feeds the soil and stimulates plant life.

We sometimes refer to fertilizing as feeding plants. We should think of adding compost as feeding the soil. In a small handful of compost-rich soil there are literally billions and billions (my apologies to Carl Sagan) of microbial organisms: things like fungi, bacteria, actinomycetes and protozoa that feed on the organic matter breaking it down into humus. In the process these microbes release nutrients, secrete glues that help the soil form a crumbly structure, and do a host of other things that benefit plant life.

Like the microbes in a cow's stomach can turn grass into the nutrients that amount to "cow food," microbes in the soil turn grass, leaves, wood, bark and other organic materials into nutrients that become "plant food." To put it simply, healthy soil builds healthy plants and compost builds healthy soil.

Here in the South the soil's organic matter content stays low due in part to our warm climate. The soil microbes work overtime breaking it down. If we are to maintain a high level of organic matter we must continue to add it to the soil each year.

We can purchase compost for our gardens and landscapes or make some ourselves. Those grass clippings, leaves, branch trimmings and other materials are some of the most valuable products of our gardens and landscapes. They are truly nature's own slow-release fertilizer! Put the natural processes of mulching and composting to work in your garden. You'll be surprised just how easy and effective it can be. To learn more about how to make compost or other ways to recycle leaves and clippings back into the garden contact the Travis County Agrilife Extension Office at 512-854-9600 for a free brochure.

Skip Richter, *Distinguished Decomposer of Dead Debris*

COMPOST PILE FUNDAMENTALS

- Mix grass clippings (the green stuff) and leaves (the brown stuff) half and half by weight in an eight inch layer.

- When the bin no longer feels hot in the middle, add fresh material and water as you turn it.

- The finished compost will be a dark, rich soil-like product with an earthy aroma.

- After each layer, toss in a handful of soil or finished compost and water well.

PRUNING CALENDAR FOR ORNAMENTAL TREES AND SHRUBS

WOODY PLANT TYPE	JAN	FEB	MAR	APR	MAY	JUN	JUL	AUG	SEP	OCT	NOV	DEC
Spring Flowering Deciduous Shrubs (forsythia, spirea, mock orange, flowering quince, wisteria, viburnum)	Branches can be brought indoors for forcing into early bloom.			Shape bush after bloom. Cut shoots back to where they join a side		Pinch off tips of vigorous upright shoots as needed to encourage low branching.					Move and transplant plants to desired location.	
Summer Flowering Deciduous Shrubs (althaea, hydrangea)			Prune hydrangeas to healthy wood just after growth begins.		Pinch tips of vigorous upright growth to encourage dense anching.		After blooming, prune lightly to shape as desired.				Move and transplant plants to desired location.	
Spring Flowering Deciduous Trees (dogwood, redbud, fringe tree, star and saucer magnolias, ornamental fruit trees)	Branches can be brought indoors for forcing into early bloom.			Prune only as needed after blooming to shape and thin trees. Remove shoots sprouting from base of tree.							Move and transplant plants to desired location.	
Summer Flowering Deciduous Trees (crape myrtle, vitex)	Prune to maintain basic structure. Heavier pruning results in fewer, larger blooms.				Remove spent flowers to encourage more blooming.						Move and transplant plants to desired location.	
Deciduous Shade Trees (maple, oak, sycamore, ash, elm, pecan)	Prune to train young trees and new transplants. Remove narrow-angled scaffold limbs.			Trim lower branches as needed to allow clearance for yard work and leisure activities and to increase light intensity to maintain turf.							Move and transplant plants to desired location.	
Broad-leaved Evergreen Shrubs (ligustrum, yaupon, photinia, pittisporum	Severely cut back on overgrown shrubs to bring back into bounds.			Shear or trim as needed to maintain form and size. Trim to keep tops of hedges slightly more narrow than the base.							Move and transplant plants to desired location.	
Broad-leaved Evergreen Flowering Shrubs (azalea, camellia, abelia, indian hawthorne, oleander, gardenia)	Prune summer- blooming shrubs in late winter.			Prune spring-blooming shrubs *after* they bloom. Prune leggy branches back to maintain form and encourage branching.							Move and transplant plants to desired location.	
Needle-leaved Evergreen Trees and Shrubs (pine, yew, arborvitae, juniper)	Prune as necessary for correction and repair.		Shape new growth before new wood forms. Pinch out tips of pine shoots to encourage branching as needed.			Lightly shear hedges to maintain shape. Remove dead and diseased branches to discourage spread of diseases. Avoid cutting pine branches back beyond where green needles are growing.					Move and transplant plants to desired location.	

FEBRUARY

1	
2	
3	
4	
5	
6	
7	
8	
9	
10	
11	
12	
13	
14	
15	
16	
17	
18	
19	
20	
21	
22	
23	
24	
25	
26	
27	
28	
[29]	

/garden notes

PRUNING GUIDE

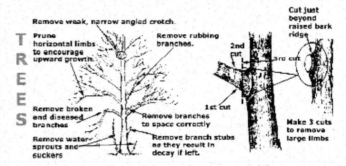

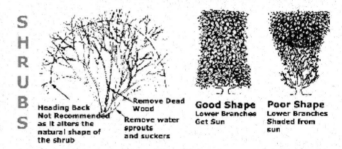

OTHER THINGS TO DO

Time to get the garden ready for the new spring growing season. Clean, repair and replace garden tools. Complete garden plan to help organize your chores and planting schedules. Have lawnmower blade sharpened and the oil changed.

PRUNE: Prune evergreen shrubs, shade and fruit trees (best time is just before bud break), summer and fall-flowering shrubs. Do not prune spring-flowering shrubs such as azaleas, spirea and philadelphus (mock orange); they've already set blooms. Prune roses around Valentine's Day, except climbers and other "once bloomers". Prune *after* flowering. Prune grape vines and trim sides of blackberry rows to keep neat and pickable. Mow straggly groundcovers on high setting to renew the planting.

Holidays/ Observations this Month:
Groundhog Day, Valentine's Day, President's Day

THINGS TO PLANT IN FEBRUARY

FLOWER PLANTS: African Daisy (Arctotis), Alyssum, Summer Forget-Me-Not (Anchusa), Snapdragon (Antirrhinum), English Daisy (Bellis), Balloon Flower, Butterfly Weed, Calendula, Candytuft, Coneflower, Chrysanthemum, Cornflower, Delphinium, Dianthus, Daisy (African, Michaelmas and Painted), Feverfew, Gaillardia, Larkspur, Liatris, Edging Lobelia, Cardinal Flower (Lobelia), Monkey Flower (Mimulus), Nasturtium, Penstemon, Ornamental Cabbage and Kale, Pansy, Phlox (drummondii and paniculata), Stock, Johnny-Jump-Up and Pansy (Viola).

FLOWER SEEDS: Alyssum, Calendula, Candytuft, Cosmos, Flowering Tobacco (Nicotiana), Four O' Clock, Gayfeather, Larkspur, Linaria, Marigold, Monkey Flower, Nasturtium, Penstemon, Petunia, Phlox (drummondii), Salvia, Stock (Dwarf), Verbena, Sweet Pea, Sweet William (Dianthus).

BULBS: Agapanthus, Amaryllis (in containers), Allium, Alstroemeria, Amarcrinum, Calla, Canna, Crinum, Dahlia, Daylily, Gladiolus, Spider Lily (Hymerocallis), Liriope, Monkey Grass, Mondo Grass, Rainlily, Society Garlic, Tigridia, Tulip.

VEGETABLES:
Early—Mid Month: Asparagus crowns, Broccoli plants, Cabbage plants, Cauliflower plants, Carrots, Chard, Onion bulbs, Peas (English & edible pod), Potato (Irish), Spinach.
Mid—Late Month: Mustard.
All Month: Beets, Collards, Kohlrabi, Lettuce, Radish, Turnip.

HERBS: Dill, Fennel, Garlic Chives, Horseradish, Lemon Balm, Mint, Parsley, Rosemary, Summer Savory.

FRUIT: Bare root or container grown Pecans, Fruit trees, Grapes and Berry bushes.

THINGS TO DO IN FEBRUARY

FERTILIZE: Feed winter bloomers such as alyssum, dianthus and especially pansies. Fertilize maidenhair fern with bone meal.

WATER: Water everything well before a freeze, but avoid overwatering.

TRANSPLANT: Plant bare root and container grown roses, shrubs, trees, groundcovers and vines. Move hardy seedlings outdoors. Divide and transplant perennial herbs and summer and fall blooming perennial flowers. Donate extras to a plant sale.

PREPARE SOIL: Add compost and/or fertilizer. Loosen the soil. Send in soil samples (forms available at the Travis County Agrilife Extension Office). Check winter mulch and replenish if needed. Stockpile leaves for mulch and composting throughout spring and summer.

LAWN CARE: If lawn has a history of brown patch problems, treat with a labeled fungicide late in the month. Repeat treatment in three to four weeks, if needed.

DISEASES/PESTS TO LOOK FOR: Apply pre-emergent weed killer to lawn. Spray fruit trees with dormant oil just prior to bud break. Call Travis County Agrilife Extension Office at 512-854-9600 for fruit and nut tree spray schedules, if spraying not done in January.

Need help with a Gardening Question? Call our Master Gardeners Help Desk:
512-854-9600 Monday-Friday, 9 am-5 pm
or visit our website: www.tcmastergardeners.org or email: travismg@ag.tamu.edu

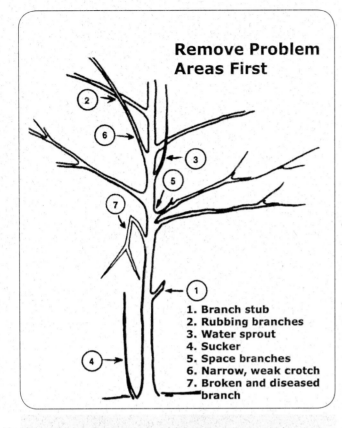

Remove Problem Areas First

1. Branch stub
2. Rubbing branches
3. Water sprout
4. Sucker
5. Space branches
6. Narrow, weak crotch
7. Broken and diseased branch

PLAN APPROACH TO PRUNING

Pruning should follow a definite plan.

Consider the reason or purpose before cutting begins. You can reduce the number of pruning cuts by making them in the right order. A skilled pruner first removes all dead, broken, diseased or problem limbs by cutting them at the point of origin or back to a strong lateral branch or shoot. Often, removing this material opens the canopy sufficiently so that no further pruning is necessary.

Next, make any training cuts that are needed.

Train the tree or shrub to develop a desired shape or fill in storm damage by cutting back to lateral branches. Keep in mind the plant's natural growth habit. Consider replacing it with a plant more appropriate for your site if frequent pruning is required.

Make additional corrective pruning cuts to eliminate weak or narrow crotches and to remove the less desirable leader where double leaders occur. After these cuts have been made, stand back and take a look at your work. Are any other corrective pruning cuts necessary? If the amount of wood removed is considerable, further pruning may need to be delayed a year or so. Remove water sprouts unless they are needed to fill a hole or to shade a large limb until other branches develop. Make the cut close to the trunk or limb so that no stubs are left and the chance of additional sprouts arising from the adventitious buds near the wound is reduced.

REASONS TO PRUNE

•Improve the chance of survival at transplanting time.

•Direct or correct growth in shade trees.

•Maintain the natural shape of the tree.

•Maintain or limit the size of a plant so that it doesn't grow out of bounds.

•Remove undesirable growth that detracts from the plant.

•Remove broken, unsightly, diseased or insect- damaged growth.

•Remove suckers or water sprouts.

•Improve future flowering and/or fruiting by removing old flowers and fruit.

•Remove rubbing branches.

•Remove existing stubs that allow diseases and insects to enter the plant.

•Develop a particular form such as a hedge, topiary or espalier.

•Produce compact growth and prevent legginess.

•Maintain maximum coloration on those plants selected for twig or stem color.

•Improve or maintain flowering by selectively removing some branches, allowing light to penetrate to the interior of the plant.

•Rejuvenate old or declining plants by removing older wood so young growth can develop.

•Increase safety to humans or property.

TREE ORGANIZATIONS/ INFO

TreeFolks, Inc., PO Box 704, Austin, Texas 78767
Phone: 512-443-LEAF   Email: admin@treefolks.org
www.treefolks.org/

Texas A&M Forest Service
txforestservice.tamu.edu/

City of Austin Oak Wilt Information
www.austintx.gov/page/oak-wilt-suppression

AUSTIN CERTIFIED ARBORISTS

For information about hiring an arborist: <u>www. treesaregood.org</u>

For a list of local arborists: www.isatexas.com/Con-sumers/Find_a_Local_Arborist.htm

Tree care tips and videos:
http://www.isatexas.com/Consumers/Customer_Tree_Care_Info.htm

TREE CARE TIPS

A properly pruned tree is like a good haircut...hardly noticeable at first glance.

1. Don't top trees.

2. Learn about the natural structure and form of the species and prune accordingly.

3. Apply the rule of thirds when pruning: Never remove more than 1/3 of a tree's crown. Where possible, encourage side branches that form 1/3 of vertical angles in 10 or 2 o'clock positions. For most deciduous (broad-leaf) trees, don't prune up from the bottom any more than 1/3 of the tree's total height. Ideally, main side branches should be at least 1/3 smaller than trunk diameter.

4. If removal of main branches is necessary, cut them back to the branch collar to avoid leaving stubs.

5. During the first 10-15 years after planting, apply 1 lb. of 15-5-10 per inch of trunk diameter throughout the area covered by the branch spread and 1/3 beyond. Fertilizer can be spread on the surface or placed in 6" deep holes spaced 2 feet apart.

ROOT NOTES

1. The framework of major roots usually lies less than 8-12 inches below the surface.

2. Because roots need oxygen, they don't normally grow in compacted oxygen-poor soil.

3. Roots often grow outward to a diameter 1 to 2 times the height of the tree.

4. Mulching root areas generously retains moisture, retards weed growth and feeds the plant when it has decomposed. Note: Avoid piling mulch around trunk of tree.

MARCH

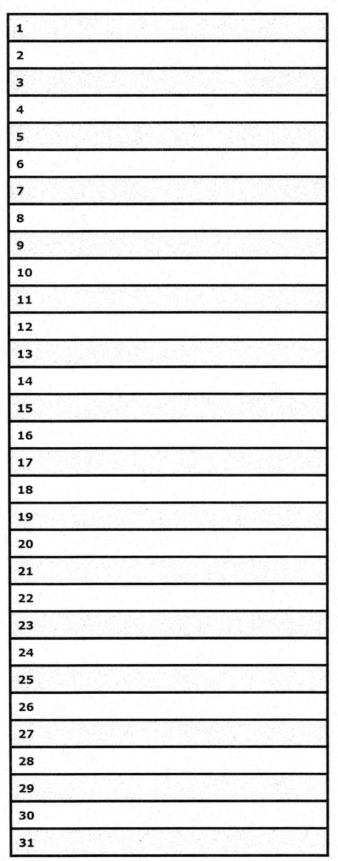

1	
2	
3	
4	
5	
6	
7	
8	
9	
10	
11	
12	
13	
14	
15	
16	
17	
18	
19	
20	
21	
22	
23	
24	
25	
26	
27	
28	
29	
30	
31	

/garden notes

Last average freeze date for our area is around March 3RD, but be prepared to protect tender plants throughout the month.

While both are celebrated on March 17th, **St. Gertrude** is usually overlooked in favor of St. Patrick. Since St. Gertrude is the patron saint of cats and gardens, her day should be honored, as well, don't you agree? So, plant some catnip for your felines and some flowers for yourself today.

TEN TIPS FOR TERRIFIC TOMATOES

1. Don't plant in the shade. Sunlight equals large, tasty fruit.
2. Prepare the site by mixing in organic matter and fertilizer.
3. Plant in raised beds—tomatoes can't swim.
4. Select locally proven varieties with a 'VFN' after their name.
5. Plant at least three varieties to hedge your bet.
6. Mulch soil to control weeds, hold moisture and reduce early disease problems.
7. Stake or cage plants to keep fruit off the ground. Staking and removing suckers makes fewer, larger, earlier fruit.
8. Feed plants weekly with a balanced fertilizer after first fruit are set. Growing, producing plants get hungry.
9. Water regularly in the heat of the summer. Deep soakings are best.
10. Inspect regularly for signs of insect and disease damage. Early control is important.

OTHER THINGS TO DO

Welcome the purple martins back to Austin! Install a new purple martin house and/or clean out existing houses.

> **Holidays/Observances this Month:** Texas Independence Day, Mardi Gras and Ash Wednesday (which change yearly with Easter Sunday date), Daylight Saving Time begins (2nd Sunday), St. Patrick's Day, St. Gertrude's Day (patron saint of cats and gardens), Vernal Equinox (Spring officially begins)

THINGS TO PLANT IN MARCH

FLOWER PLANTS: Achillea (Yarrow), Ageratum*, Alyssum, Joseph's Coat* (Amaranthus), Summer Forget-Me-Not (Anchusa), African Daisy (Arctotis), Alpine Aster, Butterfly Weed (Asclepias), Balloon Flower, Balsam*, Blue Daze*, Blue Cardinal Flower, Boltonia, Scarlet Bouvardia, Browallia*, Calliopsis, Candytuft, Chocolate Plant*, Chrysanthemum, Cigar Plant* (Cuphea ignea), Cleome*, Cockscomb*, Coleus*, Columbine, Copper Plant*, Coreopsis, Dahlia*, Dianthus, Daisy (Michaelmas, Shasta and Painted), Feverfew, Gaillardia, Geranium*, Gomphrena*, Hibiscus*, Hollyhock, Indian Blanket, Jacobinia*, Lamb's Ear (Stachys), Lantana*, Liatris, Edging Lobelia, Mexican Heather (Cuphea hyssopifolia), Nasturtium*, Nierembergia*, Penstemon, Penta, Petunia*, Phlox Drummondii, Plumbago*, Oriental Poppy, Salvia* (farinacea, greggii, leucantha, splendens), Sedum, Spiderwort (Tradescantia), Stokes' Aster, Sunflower* (Helianthus), Torenia (Wishbone Flower), Veronica.

FLOWER SEEDS: Ageratum, Balsam, Amethyst Flower (Browallia), Candytuft, Castor Bean, Cleome, Butterfly Pea (Clitoria), Cosmos, Dahlia, Echinacea, Feverfew, Impatiens, Moonflower (Ipomea alba), Cypress Vine (Ipomoea quamoclit), Gomphrena, Sunflower (Helianthus), Nasturtium, Flowering Tobacco (Nicotiana), Pinks (Dianthus), Portulaca (Moss Rose), Sweet Sultan, Marigold (Tagetes), Tithonia, Torenia, Verbena.

BULBS: Achimenes, Acidanthera, Allium, Alstroemeria, Amarcrinum, Amaryllis, Ground Orchid (Bletilla), Caladium, Calla, Canna, Crinum, Crocosmia, Dahlia, Daylily, Butterfly Iris (Dietes), Ginger, Gladiolus, Gloriosa Lily, Hosta, Spider Lily (Hymerocallis), Yellow Star Grass (Hypoxis), Liriope, Monkey Grass, Rain Lily, Society Garlic, Tigridia, Tuberose.

VEGETABLES:
Early—Mid Month: Beets, Collards, Turnip.
Mid—Late Month: Beans, Corn, Cucumber, Eggplant, Peppers, Pumpkin, Squash, Tomatoes.
All Month: Lettuce, Mustard, Radish.
Be prepared to protect plants from frosts and freezes. Give transplants a weekly boost the first month with a liquid plant food or "manure tea."

HERBS: Anise, Star Anise, Basil*, Bay, Borage, Bouncing Bet, Caraway, Catnip, Chives, Comfrey, Costmary, Cumin, Fennel, Fenugreek, Scented Geranium*, Germander, Horehound, Horseradish, Lamb's Ear, Lavender, Lemon Grass*, Lemon Verbena, Mexican Mint Marigold (a great substitute for French Tarragon), Monarda, Oregano, Parsley, Perilla, Rosemary, Sage, Santolina, Summer Savory, Winter Savory, Sesame, Sorrel, Southernwood, Tansy, Tarragon, Thyme, Common Wormwood, Roman Wormwood, Yarrow.

FRUIT: Container grown fruit and nut trees, vines and bushes.

***Plant mid-month after danger of freezing has passed.**

THINGS TO DO IN MARCH

FERTILIZE: Begin monthly feedings of hibiscus after pruning. Start a rose feeding schedule; spray and feed camellias. Begin fertilizing azaleas after they bloom. Fertilize established fruit and nut trees with 1 lb. 15-5-10 per inch of trunk diameter. Berry bushes should receive 1/3 cup per square yard of planting area.

DISEASES/PESTS TO LOOK FOR: Watch for aphids on new growth, spider mites on older leaves and cut worms on young transplants. Spray peach and plum trees for curculio weevils when 3/4 of the petals have fallen (repeat three times at two-week intervals).

PRUNE: Prune hibiscus, also spring flowering shrubs and trees, *after* they bloom. Prune and train vines. Shape spring-blooming shrubs with light pruning after bloom. Allow bulb foliage to yellow and die before removing.

FLOWERS

COOL SEASON FLOWERING

Alyssum
Bachelor's Button
California Poppy
Sweet Pea
Viola

Calendula
Candytuft
Gypsophila
Pansy
Snapdragon

WARM SEASON FLOWERING

Aster
Cosmos
Marigold
Scabiosa
Verbena
Gomphrena

Celosia
Dahlia
Salvia
Stock
Zinnia

FLOWERS FOR PARTLY-SHADY AREAS

Alyssum
Campanula
Columbine
Godetia
Lobelia
Pansy
Viola

Balsam
Coleus
Forget-Me-Not
Impatiens
Nicotiana
Sweet William

LOW GROWERS/EDGING FLOWERS

Ageratum
Blackfoot Daisy
Hymenoxys
Dwarf Marigold
Pansy
Moss Rose
Verbena
Narrow Leaf Zinnia

Alyssum
Candytuft
Lobelia
Nasturtium
Dwarf Phlox
Snapdragon
Dwarf Zinnia

TALL/BACKGROUND FLOWERS

Cleome
Delphinium
Hollyhock
Sunflower

Cosmos
Four o'clock
Larkspur

FLOWERS FOR POOR/DRY SOIL

Ageratum
Bachelor's Button
Celosia
Gaillardia

Alyssum
Blackfoot Daisy
Cosmos
Hymenoxys

Kochia
Morning Glory
Moss Rose
Verbena

Marigold
Nasturtium
Snapdragon
Vinca

FLOWERS FOR CUTTING/BOUQUETS

Aster
Bachelor's Button
Celosia
Cynoglossum
Gaillardia
Larkspur
Nasturtium
Dianthus
Snapdragon
Sweet Pea
Zinnia

Calendula
Carnation
Cosmos
Dahlia
Gypsophila
Marigold
Phlox
Scabiosa
Stock
Verbena

FRAGRANT FLOWERS

Alyssum
Moonflower
Nasturtium
Petunia
Stock
Verbena

Carnation
Morning Glory
Nicotiana
Dianthus
Sweet Pea

POPULAR PERENNIALS

Butterfly Weed
Purple Coneflower
Delphinium
Gaillardia
Hollyhock
Salvia
Sweet William
Yarrow

Columbine
Coreopsis
Forget-Me-Not
Guara
Phlox
Shasta Daisy
Viola

FLOWER TYPES

Annuals: Grow from seed and flower the first year, then die.
Perennials: Establish themselves from seed the first year, usually do not bloom until the second year, then flower for many years.
Biennials: Form a small plant the first year, bloom the second year, then die.

THESE ROSES SURVIVE WITH FEWER APPLICATIONS OF PESTICIDES

AMERICA—Climbing rose; flower SALMON COLOR, reverse lighter, double flower (43 petals), medium (3-4 inch); very fragrant.

APRICOT NECTAR— Flower PINK APRICOT COLOR, base golden, double, cupped, large (4 inch); very fragrant (fruity); foliage glossy, dark; growth vigorous and bushy. All-American Rose Society Award, 1966.

BELINDA'S ROSE—Flower ROSE PINK COLOR, double; very fragrant; foliage dark and bluish green; growth vigorous, upright and compact. This rose is available from nurseries which specialize in antique roses.

CHRYSLER IMPERIAL—Flower DEEP RED COLOR, double (45 petals), high-centered, large (5 inch); very fragrant; foliage dark, semi-glossy; Growth is vigorous and compact. All-American Rose Society Award, 1953.

DON JUAN—Climbing/self supporting rose; flower VELVETY DARK RED COLOR, double (35 petals), cupped, large (5 inch); very fragrant; foliage dark, glossy, leathery; 8 feet tall.

DOUBLE DELIGHT—Flower CREAMY WHITE BECOMING STRAWBERRY-RED COLOR, double bloom (40 petals), high centered, large (5 inch); fragrant (spicy); growth upright, spreading, bushy. All-American Rose Society Award, 1977. Rose Fragrance Medal, 1986.

FRAGRANT CLOUD—Flower CORAL-RED BECOMING GERANIUM-RED COLOR, double (28 petals), well-formed, large (5 inch); very fragrant; foliage dark, glossy; growth vigorous and upright. Fragrance Medal, 1969.

GOLD MEDAL—Flower DEEP GOLDEN YELLOW COLOR, double (38 petals), classic shape, opening formal, spiraled; fragrance (light tea); foliage large, dark; growth tall, upright, bushy.

MISTER LINCOLN—Flower DARK RED COLOR, double flower (35 petals), high-centered to cupped, large bloom (5 inch); very fragrant; foliage leathery, dark; growth vigorous. All-American Rose Society Award, 1965.

NEW DAWN—Climbing rose; flower CAMEO PINK FADING WHITE COLOR, double, large; fragrant; foliage dark and glossy.

PRISTINE—Flower NEAR WHITE, SHADED LIGHT PINK COLOR, double flowered (28 petals), large bloom (5 inch); slightly fragrant; foliage very large and dark; growth upright.

QUEEN ELIZABETH—Flower MEDIUM PINK COLOR, double flower (38 petals), high-centered to cupped, large (4 inch) blooms borne singly and in clusters; fragrant; foliage dark, glossy, leathery; growth very vigorous, upright and bushy. All-American Rose Society Award, 1955.

OLD/ANTIQUE ROSES

Old garden rose varieties recommended for the Austin area include:

- **Archduke Charles**
- **Champney's Pink Cluster**
- **Duchesse de Brabant**
- **Knockout**
- **Marie Pavie**
- **Marchesa Boccella**
- **Martha Gonzales**
- **Mrs. B. R. Cant**
- **Mrs. Dudley Cross**
- **Nearly Wild**
- **Old Blush**
- **Paul Neyron**
- **Souvenir de la Malmaison**

For free advice and answers to your rose growing questions, contact the following Austin Rose Society Consulting Rosarians:

512-836-4679 - Don and Patricia Freeman

Austin Rose Society
Meeting: 3rd Tuesday of the month, 7:30 pm at Zilker Garden Center, 2220 Barton Springs Road, Austin, TX 78746
http://www.austinrosesociety.org

Visit the American Rose Society:
www.ars.org
Earthkind Rose Information:
http://aggie-horticulture.tamu.edu/earthkindroses/

A Noted Supplier of Old/Antique Roses:
The Antique Rose Emporium
10000 FM 50
Brenham, TX 77833
1-800-441-0002
www.antiqueroseemporium.com

For more information:
Antique Roses for The South
William C. Welch, Neil Sperry (1990)

Roses in the Southern Garden
G. Michael Shoup, Felder Rushing (2000)

The Organic Rose Garden
Liz Druitt, Virginia Brown (Photographer) (1996)

APRIL

1	
2	
3	
4	
5	
6	
7	
8	
9	
10	
11	
12	
13	
14	
15	
16	
17	
18	
19	
20	
21	
22	
23	
24	
25	
26	
27	
28	
29	
30	

/garden notes

SPRING PLANTED BULBS
(Recommended Planting Depth)

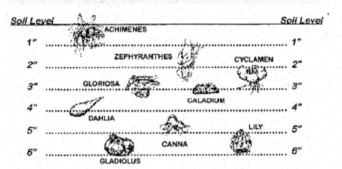

CONSERVE LANDSCAPE WATER BY FOLLOWING THESE RULES

- Use good design principles.
- Thoroughly prepare beds.
- Limit irrigated turf areas.
- Make effective use of mulch materials.
- Choose native or drought tolerant plants.
- Practice smart general garden maintenance.

DISEASES/PESTS TO LOOK FOR: Spray roses with fungicide to prevent blackspot. Continue spraying peach and plum trees for curculio. Call The Travis County Agrilife Extension Office (512-854-9600) for spray schedule for fruit and nut trees. Watch for stinkbugs and early blight on tomatoes.

PRUNE: Prune spring-flowering shrubs and trees *after* they bloom. Prune climbing roses and other "once bloomers" as soon as they finish flowering. Divide chrysanthemums and pinch tips for bushier growth. Thin peaches 4 to 6 inches apart and plums 3 to 4 inches apart. Thin apples and pears to one per cluster.

Holidays/Observances this month:
April Fool's Day, National Arbor Day

 Arbor Day Foundation™

THINGS TO PLANT IN APRIL

FLOWER PLANTS: Ageratum, Ajuga, Joseph's Coat (Amaranthus), Balsam, Wax Begonia, Blue Daze, Blue Cardinal Flower, Boltonia, Scarlet Bouvardia, Calico Plant, Chocolate Plant, Cigar Plant (Cuphea Ignea), Cockscomb, Coleus, Columbine, Coneflower (Echinacea), Copper Plant, Coreopsis, Cosmos sulphureus, Dahlia, Shasta Daisy, Feverfew, Geranium, Gomphrena, Hibiscus, Hollyhock, Impatiens, Jacobinia, Lantana, Marigold (African, French and Mexican Mint), Nierembergia, Penta, Periwinkle, Persian Shield, Plumbago, Phlox drummondii, Portulaca, Purslane, Rudbeckia hirta, Salvia, Sedum, Stokes' Aster, Sunflower (Helianthus), Wishbone Flower (Torenia), Yarrow, Zinnia.

FLOWER SEEDS: Ageratum, Balsam, Castor Bean, Celosia, Cleome, Cockscomb, Coleus, Coral Vine, Cosmos, Cypress Vine, Dahlia (Dwarf), Coneflower (Echinacea), Feverfew, Four-o'clock, Globe Amaranth, Gourd, Impatiens, Linaria, Nasturtium, Marigold, Moonflower, Morning Glory, Periwinkle, Petunia, Pinks, Portulaca, Scabiosa, Sunflower, Sweet Pea (Perennial), Tithonia, Torenia, Vinca, Zinnia.

BULBS: Achimenes, Acidanthera, Allium, Alstroemeria, Amarcrinum, Amaryllis, Ground Orchid (Bletilla), Caladium, Calla, Canna, Crinum, Dahlia, Daylily, Dietes, Ginger, Gladiolus, Gloriosa Daisy, Hosta, Spider Lily (Hymerocallis), Hypoxis, Liriope, Monkey Grass, Rain Lily, Society Garlic, Tigridia.

VEGETABLES:
ALL Month: Amaranth, Bean, Corn, Cucumber, Eggplant, Muskmelon, Okra, Peanut, Pepper, Pumpkin, Southern Pea, Squash, Sweet Potato, Tomatillo, Tomato, Watermelon.

HERBS: Anise, Star Anise, Basil, Bay, Borage, Bouncing Bet, Caraway, Catnip, Chives, Comfrey, Costmary, Cumin, Fennel, Fenugreek, Scented Geranium, Germander, Horehound, Horseradish, Lamb's Ear, Lavender, Lemon Grass, Lemon Verbena, Mexican Mint Marigold (a great substitute for French Tarragon), Monarda, Oregano, Perilla, Rosemary, Sage, Santolina, Summer Savory, Winter Savory, Sesame, Sorrel, Southernwood, Tansy, Tarragon, Thyme, Common Wormwood, Roman Wormwood, Yarrow.

FRUIT: Bare root or container grown Pecans, Fruit trees, Grapes and Berry bushes.

THINGS TO DO IN APRIL

FERTILIZE: Tomatoes and peppers should be fed with a liquid fertilizer. Feed crape myrtle beneath the branch spread with 1/3 cup complete fertilizer per sq. yd. After second mowing, fertilize lawn with 3-1-2 ratio product; aerate first, if needed. Fertilize all houseplants with complete fertilizer. After blooming, feed bulbs with bone meal. Mulch trees, shrubs, vegetable garden and flower beds (after soil has warmed) with 2-4 inches of mulch. Pine needles and oak leaves make a good mulch for acid-loving plants. Spread coffee grounds around azaleas and other acid-loving plants.

WATER: Water as needed.

TRANSPLANT: Divide and transplant late summer- and fall-flowering bulbs. Container-grown plants (almost any kind) can go into the ground now. Plant summer annuals to get their root systems established before the extreme heat arrives.

LAWN CARE: Plant grass sod or plugs. Water daily for one or two weeks to establish. Begin regular lawn care. Mow every 5-7 days, leaving the clippings on the lawn. Keep St. Augustine grass at 2-1/2 to 3 inches.

Need help with a Gardening Question? Call our Master Gardeners Help Desk:
512-854-9600 Monday-Friday, 9 am-5 pm
or visit our website: www.tcmastergardeners.org or email: travismg@ag.tamu.edu

Butterflies add a new dimension to your landscape. Their brilliant colors flashing in the sun will bring a smile to any gardener's face. Butterflies are second only to bees as plant pollinators. Their life cycle from egg to caterpillar to chrysalis to adult butterfly is an indicator of a healthy environment.

Creating a butterfly garden is exciting and rewarding. By gardening with their needs in mind, you will attract butterflies to your area to enjoy all year 'round. Here are some useful guidelines:

Location: Locate the garden in a sunny area. Butterflies are cold blooded and need sun to warm their flight muscles. Most of the nectar plants do best in full sun.

Plant Selection: Plant flowers that produce nectar. Butterflies visit flowers in search of this sugary fluid as a source of nutrition.

Single flowers: The nectar of single flowers is more accessible and easier for butterflies to extract.

Splashes of color: Butterflies are first attracted to flowers by their color. Groups of flowers such as six to twelve zinnias are easier for butterflies to locate than a single isolated plant. Red/orange colors are preferred by many butterflies.

Continuous bloom: Plan for various flowers to be in bloom throughout the growing season. In Travis County, butterflies are active from spring through fall and even on warm sunny winter days you'll find lots of activity. In the spring plant: Zinnia, Verbena, Asters. In the summer: Lantana, Penta, Tithonia and Buddleia. In the fall: Blue Mist Flower.

Host plants: Include host plants in your garden design. Host plants provide food for caterpillars and lure females into the garden to lay eggs. Females are very specific and will lay eggs only on host plants desirable to her offspring.

Moisture: Include damp areas in your garden. Some butterflies drink and extract minerals from the soil.

Tanning booth: Place flat stones in the garden. Butterflies often perch on stones, bare soil or vegetation, spread their wings and bask in the sun. This raises their body temperature so they are able to fly and remain active.

Pesticide free: Do not use pesticides in or near the butterfly garden. Most traditional garden pesticides are toxic to butterflies. Use predatory insects or insecticidal soap or remove the pest by hand if problems occur.

After mating, female butterflies search for their specific host plant on which to lay eggs. In a few days, caterpillars emerge from the eggs and begin to eat. They are selective eaters and only feed on specific plants. If the desired plants are not available, they will starve rather than eat another type of plant. Most butterflies are not considered agricultural pests. The caterpillars can be expected to eat large amounts of the host plant's vegetation. For example, expect the Gulf Fritillary to strip a passion vine. Eastern Black Swallowtails will denude dill plants. Plan on this, and grow six plants for the butterflies and two plants for your own use.

In a few weeks when the caterpillars are fully grown, they will shed their skin for the last time and change into a chrysalis. Inside each chrysalis, the body of an adult butterfly is formed. Often the chrysalis is attached to a piece of plant stem and is hidden by the surrounding vegetation. After emerging from the chrysalis, the adult butterfly will take a few minutes to an hour to dry off. Once the wings are dry, the newly emerged adult will fly off in search of nectar- rich flowers from which to feed.

FOR MORE INFORMATION CONTACT:
Austin Butterfly Forum, Inc.
www.austinbutterflies.org

Butterflies and Moths of North America:
www.butterfliesandmoths.org

BOOKS ABOUT BUTTERFLIES:
Butterflies of West Texas Parks and Preserves by Roland H. Wauer (2002)
Butterflies of Houston & Southeast Texas (Corrie Herring Hooks Series, No. 32) by John L. Tveten, Gloria Tveten (Contributor) (1996)
Butterfly Gardening for Texas by Geyata Ajilvsgi (2013)

HOST PLANTS/FAVORITE NECTAR PLANTS FOR TEN BUTTERFLIES IN TRAVIS COUNTY

Host Plants	Butterfly	Nectar Plants
	Black Swallowtail	
Dill, Fennel, Parsley		Zinnia, Gaillardia
	Dogface	
Legumes, Kidneywood		Cardinal Flower, Zinnia
	Giant Swallowtail	
Wafer Ash, Rue		Lantana, Buddleia, Penta
	Gulf Fritillary	
Passion Vine		Lantana, Buddleia, Penta
	Hackberry	
Hackberry tree		Fruit tree blossoms, Lantana
	Julia Longwing	
Passion Vine		Tithonia, Golden-eye
	Monarch	
Mexican Milkweed		Lantana, Verbena, Milkweed
	Painted Lady	
Thistle, Artemesia		Sunflower, Tithonia
	Pipevine Swallowtail	
Native Pipevine		Fruit tree blossoms, Lantana
	Texas Crescent Spot	
Flame Acanthus		Kidneywood, Englemann Daisy

WATER GARDENING

PLANTING THE POND

Planting the pond is the most exciting time and one of the most crucial. Spring is the best time to complete this task. Plants bought for the pond should be in top condition and installed immediately upon receipt, if possible. Therefore, do not purchase the plants until you are ready to plant, or if ordering through the mail, plan their arrival carefully. Many mail order dealers ship their plants at only certain times of the year.

Plants bought from a garden center are often potted and ready to be placed in the pond. If not, or if you purchase your plants from mail order houses, they will come to you bare root, wrapped in plastic containing a moist, organic medium or paper. These plants should be removed from the medium, washed and potted immediately upon receipt. Plan ahead and have your soil, fertilizer tablets, pots and burlap, if you are using baskets, ready ahead of time.

Lilies (Nymphaea): Tropical lilies form crowns and should be planted in deep pots. The crown should be placed in the soil and covered with one inch of gravel on top, leaving the growing point above the soil and gravel.

Hardy lilies grow from rhizomes and should be grown in wide shallow tubs or baskets. The rhizome should be placed in the soil at a 45° angle and covered with soil and 1 inch of gravel. Be sure to leave the growing tip above the soil and gravel.

Tropical and hardy water lilies should be covered with 6 to 18 inches of water.

Lotus (Nelumbo): Water lotus should be considered bog plants, as they do not contribute to covering the surface of the pond as do the floating leafed water lilies. Water lotus grow from large vigorous banana-shaped rhizomes and must have at least two nodes (the pinched looking area of the rhizomes) left on them when divided in order to survive. Their roots are brittle and can easily be broken, killing the plant. Lotus should be grown in large tubs or baskets no less than 32 quarts in size. Place the rhizomes shallowly in the pot and cover with soil and 1 inch of gravel. It may be necessary to put a rock or brick over the tubers of these plants until rooted to prevent them from floating out of the soil. Lotus should be placed in the pond about 4 inches below the water surface. To place the lotus in deeper portions of the pond, put them up on blocks or bricks to achieve the proper depth. Place scraps of liner under the bricks to guard against punctures.

Oxygenators: These plants often arrive in bundles of cuttings and should be planted as they are into pots and placed on the bottom of the pond. Their roots are merely for anchorage so they can be placed in sand, soil or gravel.

Bog plants: These plants should be placed in pails or pots on the shelves of the pond where the crowns of the plants are covered by about 1 inch of water.

Floating Plants: These plants should be rinsed well before placing them directly into the pond.

FISH AND WILDLIFE

Fish: Fish are not necessary for the balance of the pond, but their presence will greatly increase the speed with which it is established. They eat mosquito larvae and many other undesirable visitors to your pond, keep submerged plants pruned, recycle nutrients in the system, and add immeasurably to the beauty of the pond. Fish should be stocked at a rate no more than 1 inch of fish per 3 to 5 gallons of water in the pond. Fish attain a greater size, do less damage to submerged plants and remain healthier if stocked at rates below the capacity of the pond. Thus a small circular pond 5 feet in diameter and 18 inches deep holding around 160 gallons of water will accommodate from four to five 10 inch fish. When first introducing fish to the pond, put the fish still inside their sealed bag into the pond allowing 15 minutes for the temperature to equalize between the bag and the pond before releasing the fish. On a sunny day, cover the bag to prevent overheating.

Koi: Japanese koi are carp. These fish are generally expensive, range in mature size from 2 to 3 feet, come in many colors and live for a very long time. Koi are best suited to ponds larger than 6 feet minimum diameter and at least 24 inches deep and require high quality filtration systems.

Goldfish: They are smaller and by far the most popular fish for pond use. They are less expensive, come in many colors and range from 10 to 12 inches at maturity. Goldfish will breed in the pond, increasing in numbers over a period of years. This may present a problem for small ponds.

Frogs: Frogs are good for the pond; they supply tadpoles which are efficient scavengers and food for fish and dragonfly larvae. Also, the adults, in conjunction with the fish, control the mosquitoes and other insect problems.

For more information:
The Austin Pond Society
www.austinpondsociety.org

MAY

1	
2	
3	
4	
5	
6	
7	
8	
9	
10	
11	
12	
13	
14	
15	
16	
17	
18	
19	
20	
21	
22	
23	
24	
25	
26	
27	
28	
29	
30	
31	

/garden notes

WHY GROW GREEN?

Help Protect Water Quality
Look for earth-wise labels on gardening products at participating retailers.

The Grow Green™ program aims to educate Austin area residents on the least toxic approach to pest management and responsible fertilizer use in order to reduce the amount of landscape chemicals that "run-off" into our waterways and degrade our water quality. Call 512-854-9600 (Travis County Agrilife Extension) or 512-974-2581 (City of Austin Watershed Protection) for more information or www.austintexas.gov/department/grow-green

SPRING PLANTED, SUMMER FLOWERING ANNUALS

Alyssum-Fragrant
Amaranthus-Brilliant foliage
Bachelor Button-Attractive cut or dried flowers
Begonia-Attractive foliage and flowers
Caladium-Bright foliage, plant from tubers
Cockscomb-Crested and plume types available
Coleus-Colorful foliage
Copper Plant-Brilliant copper-colored foliage
Geranium-Needs shade during summer months
Impatiens-Bright flowers, many varieties
Lantana-Trailing, upright form; many colors
Marigold-Spider mites a problem, holds up in heat
Periwinkle-Excellent heat tolerant selection
Petunia-Many varieties
Portulaca-Excellent heat tolerance
Salvia-Needs shade during summer months
Verbena-Excellent heat tolerant selection
Zinnia-Many colors, heat resistant

Holidays/Observances this month:
May Day, Mother's Day (second Sunday of the month), Armed Forces Day, Memorial Day

THINGS TO PLANT IN MAY

FLOWER PLANTS: Ageratum, Ajuga, Joseph's Coat (Amaranthus), Balsam, Wax Begonia, Blue Daze, Blue Cardinal Flower, Boltonia, Scarlet Bouvardia, Calico Plant, Chocolate Plant, Cigar Plant (Cuphea Ignea), Cockscomb, Coleus, Columbine, Copper Plant, Coreopsis, Cosmos sulphureus, Dahlia, Shasta Daisy, Feverfew, Geranium, Gomphrena, Hibiscus, Hollyhock, Impatiens, Jacobinia, Lantana, Marigold (African, French and Mexican Mint), Nierembergia, Penta, Periwinkle, Persian Shield, Plumbago, Phlox drummondii, Portulaca, Purslane, Purple Coneflower (Echinacea), Rudbeckia Hirta, Salvia, Sedum, Stokes' Aster, Sunflower (Helianthus), Wishbone Flower (Torenia), Yarrow, Zinnia.

FLOWER SEEDS: Ageratum, Balsam, Castor Bean, Celosia, Cleome, Cockscomb, Coleus, Coral Vine, Cosmos, Cypress Vine, Dahlia (Dwarf), Echinacea, Feverfew, Four-o'clock, Globe Amaranth, Gourd, Impatiens, Linaria, Nasturtium, Marigold, Moonflower, Morning Glory, Periwinkle, Petunia, Pinks, Portulaca, Scabiosa, Sunflower, Sweet Pea (Perennial), Tithonia, Torenia, Vinca, Zinnia.

BULBS: Acidanthera, Amarcrinum, Amaryllis, Aspidistra, Caladium, Canna, Ginger, Daylily, Gladiolus, Liriope, Monkey Grass, Neomarica.

VEGETABLES:
ALL Month: Amaranth, Jerusalem Artichoke (Sunchoke), Jicama, Malabar Spinach, Okra, Southern Pea, Peanut, Pumpkin, Sweet Potato, Tomatillo, Water Spinach, Watermelon.

HERBS: Anise, Star Anise, Basil, Bay, Borage, Bouncing Bet, Caraway, Catnip, Chives, Comfrey, Costmary, Cumin, Fennel, Fenugreek, Scented Geranium, Germander, Horehound, Horseradish, Lamb's Ear, Lavender, Lemon Grass, Lemon Verbena, Mexican Mint Marigold (a great substitute for French Tarragon), Monarda, Oregano, Perilla, Rosemary, Sage, Santolina, Summer Savory, Winter Savory, Sesame, Sorrel, Southernwood, Tansy, Tarragon, Thyme, Common Wormwood, Roman Wormwood, Yarrow.

FRUIT: Container-grown plants can go in the ground.

THINGS TO DO IN MAY

FERTILIZE: Feed all spring-blooming shrubs after they have bloomed. Feed amaryllis after they bloom. Feed and mulch iris. Feed crape myrtle with 1/2 cup/sq. yd. of 3-1-2 ratio fertilizer beneath the branch spread.

WATER: Water annuals as needed. Mulch all bare soil to retain moisture.

TRANSPLANT: Container-grown plants can go into the ground now.

LAWN CARE: Mow every 5-7 days, leaving the clippings on the lawn. Keep St. Augustine grass at 2 1/2" to 3" height. Apply 1/2' to 1" of water as needed to wet soil thoroughly. Don't water more often than every five days.

DISEASES/PESTS TO LOOK FOR: Check for aphids and spider mites. Look for tobacco hornworms, spider mites and stink bugs, especially in vegetable gardens. Spray peach and plum trees for curculio weevils. Spray blackspot-susceptible roses with fungicide every 7-10 days.

PRUNE: Prune spring-flowering shrubs and trees *after* they bloom. Prune climbing roses and other "once bloomers" as soon as they finish flowering. Divide chrysanthemums and pinch tips for bushier growth. Pinch back leggy annuals to encourage branching. Deadhead plants to encourage blooming. Prune frost-damaged trees and shrubs. Remove sucker shoots from tomato plants to get earlier, larger fruit.

YEAR 'ROUND LAWN CARE

REDUCED FERTILIZER RECOMMENDATIONS

1. Test Your soil.
2. If your soil test shows:
Low to Very Low Nitrogen: Use 1/2 lb Nitrogen per 1,000 square feet two times per year.
Moderate Nitrogen: Use 1/2 lb Nitrogen per 1,000 square feet one time per year
High Nitrogen: DO NOT FERTILIZE
3. Do not bag grass clippings. Make mulch/compost.
4. Certified organic and other natural fertilizers out-performed inorganic ones in a recent study.
5. Choose a fertilizer with low phosphorous such as 9-1-1 or 6-1-1, 8-2-4, etc.

Fertilizer Analysis on Bag (%N-%P-%K)	Amount of Fertilizer needed to supply 1/2 pound of nitrogen/1000 square feet
6-1-1*	8 pounds fertilizer/1000 sq. ft.
8-2-4*	6 pounds fertilizer/1000 sq. ft.
9-1-1*	5.5 pounds fertilizer/1000 sq. ft.
12-4-8	4 pounds fertilizer/1000 sq. ft.
20-5-10	2.5 pounds fertilizer/1000 sq. ft.
21-0-0	2.5 pounds fertilizer/1000 sq. ft.

*Locally available certified organic or natural fertilizers.

RECOMMENDED TURF VARIETIES FOR AUSTIN AND VICINITY

Bermuda grass
Good drought tolerance; produces dense turf; poor shade tolerance; seeded or sodded. Varieties: Baby and Tif 419.

Buffalo grass
Excellent drought tolerance; produces thin turf; poor shade tolerance; seeded or sodded. Variety: 609.

St. Augustine grass
Produces dense turf; good shade tolerance; poor drought tolerance; sodded. Variety: Raleigh.

Zoysia grass
Produces dense turf; good shade tolerance, good drought tolerance; sodded. Varieties: Emerald, El Toro and Jamur and Palisades.

Habiturf®
Drought-tolerant native lawn developed by The Johnson Wildflower Center. www.wildflower.org/habiturf/

For more information on Turfgrass Management and Use
www.aggie-turf.tamu.edu/answers4you

> **Read carefully and follow all label directions for pesticides, herbicides, fungicides and fertilizers. Use only the recommended amounts. More is not better and may harm your plants, animals, the environment and you.**

SCHEDULE FOR LAWN CARE

Late January: An application of Daconil or Terraclor may be applied now to prevent brown patch. Re-treat 3-4 weeks later if necessary.

February: Mid Month: If lawn has a history of weed problems, apply pre-emergent herbicide now to prevent warm season annual weeds.

Late Month: Control cool season broadleaf weeds now, before they go to seed, with a post-emergent herbicide.

Mid-April: Fertilize lawn with an appropriate product. See chart above for application rates.

Summer Months: Daily lawn sprinkling encourages shallow rooting and promotes diseases. Apply 1/2" to 1" of water every 5 days to wet the soil deeply and develop a strong, healthy turf. Use a container with straight sides as a rain gauge to determine how long it takes to apply one inch.

Late Spring-Summer: Set mower higher. Taller grass encourages deeper rooting, better drought tolerance and better cover in shady areas.

June-August: Watch for chinch bugs in the sunny parts of your lawn, especially near the streets and driveways. Call the Travis County Agrilife Extension Office 512-854-9600 for recommended treatments.

Late July: If you have a significant white grub infestation, call the Travis County Agrilife Extension Office 512-854-9600 for recommended treatments.

September: Early Month: If lawn has a history of cool season weed problems, apply pre-emergent herbicide now to prevent cool season annual weeds.

Late Month: An application of Daconil or Terraclor may be applied now to prevent brown patch. Retreating 3-4 weeks later may be necessary.

Early-Mid October: Fertilize with an appropriate product. See chart, above.

Late Fall-Winter: The easiest and most efficient way to manage fallen leaves is to mow over them with a mulching lawn mower, shredding the leaves into tiny pieces which fall between the grass blades. Shredded leaves help mulch your lawn over the winter without shading it from sunlight. If you have a newer bagging mower, it can be fitted with a mulching attachment. For older model mowers, raise the front end of the mower an inch higher than the rear and close off the discharge chute. During mild winters, it may be necessary to continue treatments to prevent brown patch.

Natural Enemies of Common Garden Pests

 Trichogramma Wasp

 Syrphid Fly

 Pirate Bug

 Big-eyed Bug

 Damsel Fly

 **Green Lacewing**

 Convergent Ladybeetle

COMMON GARDEN VEGETABLE PESTS

 Blister Beetle

 Colorado Potato Beetle

 Cowpea Curculio

 Spotted Cucumber Beetle

 Flea Beetle

 White Grub

 Leaf Beetle

 **Wireworm**

 Army Worm

 **Cabbage Looper**

 Cutworm

 Corn Earworm

 Melon- worm

 **Saltmarsh Caterpillar**

 Squash Vine Borer

 Tomato Hornworm

 Mole Cricket

 Aphid

 Fleahopper

 Leafhopper

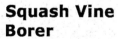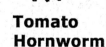

Many insects play a beneficial role for plants in the landscape. Honey bees and other pollinators are involved in the reproductive growth phase of plants and flowers. We are extremely dependent on this group of insects for the development of fruits and seeds.

There are also a number of insect predators that can attack harmful pests in the landscape. Most gardeners prize ladybugs and the occasional praying mantis for their ability to devour pesty critters. However, there are also a number of parasitic wasps, as well as nematodes, that have beneficial attributes. Other insect friends include: ground beetles, predatory mites, spiders and wasps.

Protecting these natural pest enemies is an important part of maintaining an environmentally-friendly landscape. Best way to do this: Limit pesticide use. Provide host and nectar plants for these predators. Tolerate some insect damage. Handpick critters. Use soapy water spray and other less toxic items. Learn to distinguish the good bugs from the bad.

BOOKS:

Texas Bug Book: The Good, the Bad, and the Ugly by Malcolm Beck, et al.

A Field Guide to Common TEXAS INSECTS by Bastiaan Drees, John Jackman

A Field Guide to Texas Critters: Common Household and Garden Pests by Bill Zak

The Organic Gardener's Handbook of Natural Insect and Disease Control by Barbara Ellis, et al.

JUNE

/garden notes

DID YOU KNOW THAT LESS THAN 3 PERCENT OF ALL INSECTS ARE CONSIDERED PESTS?

The rest are either beneficial or harmless. Insects pollinate fruits and vegetables, provide food for birds, fish and other wildlife, produce useful products like honey, silk, shellac and wax, help decompose leaves, branches and other organic debris into soil-enriching humus and provide the useful service of feeding on other insects considered pests to man.

Insects are part of a complex and inter-related ecosystem. A spray applied to destroy a pest may well be destroying beneficials as well. Remember that when you kill a beneficial insect, you inherit its job.

Skip Richter,
Former Travis County Agrilife Extension Director

The best pest control is the gardener's shadow. Inspect regularly and hand pick the pests. Use a strong spray of water to dislodge unwelcome visitors. Encourage beneficial insects and birds by providing appropriate habitat. Use pesticides as a last resort.

INTEGRATED PEST MANAGEMENT

IPM (Integrated Pest Management) uses four key strategies to control pest damage while fostering environmental awareness and stewardship:

- Proper plant selection (choose plants with genetic resistance to pests and disease).
- Biological control (use one organism to control another).
- Environmental and cultural controls (encourage conditions that are favorable for the plant, unfavorable for the pest).
- Chemical control (the last resort).

Holidays/Observances this month:
Father's Day (third Sunday of the month), Flag Day, Emancipation Day (Juneteenth), Summer Solstice (Summer Begins)

1	
2	
3	
4	
5	
6	
7	
8	
9	
10	
11	
12	
13	
14	
15	
16	
17	
18	
19	
20	
21	
22	
23	
24	
25	
26	
27	
28	
29	
30	

THINGS TO PLANT IN JUNE

FLOWER PLANTS: Ajuga, Balsam, Wax Begonia, Blue Daze, Boltonia, Chocolate Plant, Chrysanthemum, Cockscomb, Copper Plant, Cosmos sulphureus, Gomphrena, Hibiscus, Periwinkle, Portulaca, Purslane, Gloriosa Daisy (Rudbeckia Hirta), Salvia, Sedum, Stokes' Aster, Wishbone Flower (Torenia), Zinnia.

FLOWER SEEDS: Balsam, Blue Lace Flower, Castor Bean, Celosia, Cleome, Cockscomb, Coleus, Cosmos, Cypress Vine, Dahlia (Dwarf), Feverfew, Four-o'clock, Blanket Flower (Gaillardia), Impatiens, Marigold, Moonflower, Morning Glory, Periwinkle, Portulaca, Sunflower, Tithonia, Torenia, Vinca, Zinnia.

BULBS: Amaryllis, Canna, Crinum, Ginger, Daylily, Liriope, Monkey Grass, Rain Lily.

VEGETABLES:
ALL Month: Malabar Spinach, Okra, Southern Pea, Sweet Potato, Peanut, Pumpkin.
Start transplants indoors for fall Tomatoes, Peppers and Eggplants.

THINGS TO DO IN JUNE

FERTILIZE: Fertilize annuals with 1 cup of balanced fertilizer per 100 sq.ft. Rich compost, manure tea and fish emulsion are some organic options. Yellowing leaves near the tip of plant shoots indicate a lack of iron. Check soil pH and treat with an iron supplement, if needed. Feed roses and young fruit trees with a nitrogen fertilizer. Feed established annuals and perennials with a high nitrogen/low phosphorus fertilizer such as 15-5-10, 8-2-4 or 9-1-1.

WATER: Water all planted areas deeply but infrequently during dry periods. Water outdoor potted plants daily.

LAWN CARE: Mow every 5-7 days, leaving the clippings on the lawn. Raise mower setting to reduce stress to turf in summer. Water during the cool of early morning. Avoid weed killers now that temperatures are above 85 degrees.

DISEASES/PESTS TO LOOK FOR: Watch for chinch bugs in the sunny areas of your lawn, especially near streets and driveways. Call the Travis County Agrilife Extension for recommended treatment. Webworms and other caterpillars can be treated with Bacillus thuringiensis (Bt). For scale insects, mealy bugs and spidermites, use summer oil or horticultural oil.

PRUNE: Remove spent flowers from daisies, daylilies, cannas and other summer flowers. Remove fruiting canes from blackberries after harvest. Tip prune new canes at 4' to promote branching. Prune dead and damaged wood from trees and shrubs as needed. Cut geraniums back and place in light shade. Do not prune oak trees at this time since the beetle that carries oak wilt is active now and may be attracted to any cuts you make.

OTHER THINGS TO DO

Prepare fall garden beds. Remove old winter vegetables and strawberry plants from beds. Replenish mulch.

Need help with a Gardening Question? Call our Master Gardeners Help Desk:
512-854-9600 Monday-Friday, 9 am-5 pm
or visit our website: www.tcmastergardeners.org or email: travismg@ag.tamu.edu

INTEGRATED PEST MANAGEMENT

Integrated pest management, IPM, is a philosophy of managing pests with multiple control techniques used together. IPM balances the goals of economic production and environmental stewardship when implementing control practices. Monitoring or scouting crops for the presence and abundance of pests is an important part in the decision process of IPM.

Cultural Control: Cultural control consists of a variety of management practices, such as crop rotation, cultivation, weed management, water management, and good fertilizer use that impact pest numbers. Opportunities to interrupt the life cycle of pests with fallow periods and crop rotation should be implemented. Always destroy plant debris that harbors pests. Keep weeds under control because they attract insects that may feed on your landscape or garden.

Biological Control: Biological control is the use of one organism to control another. This includes growing nectar-producing flowers that provide food for parasites, the use of Bt (instead of pesticide) and introducing beneficial insects.

Mechanical Control: Mechanical control is the use of physical means to reduce the number of insects or their damage. Mechanical methods include barriers, covers, high-pressure water sprays and hand-picking pests.

PUTTING IT ALL INTO PRACTICE

Here are a few tips and practices that should be considered for any garden:

Plant a Garden of Manageable Size: Garden size directly affects control methods that work. Hand removal of pests and swabbing pests with alcohol may not be feasible in larger gardens. The larger the garden, the more difficulty there may be to stay ahead of pest problems.

Leave the Garden Fallow before Planting: Insect pests such as white grubs, wireworms and cutworms overwinter in the soil and feed on plants. Remove these food sources during the off season to reduce pest numbers before spring planting.

Good Sanitation: Remove diseased plants to discourage re-infestation of other plants. Either trim out infected stems and fruit or, in severe cases, remove the entire plant.

Select Pest-Free Transplants: Inspect plants at the store to be sure they have no pests. Most common insect and mite pests can be found on the under surfaces of leaves. Purchase only healthy, pest-free transplants.

Select Pest-Resistant Vegetable Varieties: Some vegetable varieties are unattractive or resistant to certain pests. Planting resistant varieties adapted to your area can dramatically reduce the need for insecticides. For example, the sweet corn varieties 'Country Gentlemen', 'Silver Queen', Honey 'N Pearl' or 'Texas Honey June' are resistant to corn earworms (due to extremely tight husks) and adapted to central Texas.

PRACTICE GOOD HORTICULTURAL METHODS

Properly Prepare the Soil before Planting: Thorough tilling of the soil will kill many soil insects and provide good growing conditions for seedlings and transplants. Healthy plants will be less susceptible to severe pest damage. The composition of the soil and spring weather also affect pest populations. Soils with high organic matter are more likely to support white grubs, root maggots, pillbugs and sowbugs, even though these soils may promote better plant growth.

Keep a Weed-free Garden: Weeds supply food for insect pests. They also compete with vegetable plants for soil nutrients and water and can decrease vegetable yield considerably. Keep weeds out of the garden and keep grass mowed short around the garden to discourage insects such as grasshoppers and armyworms from moving in.

Fertilize Properly: Plants need adequate nutrients to grow well. Without them, plants may be slow growing, stunted and more susceptible to pest damage. However, using too much fertilizer can produce lush green plants that attract insects such as aphids.

Water Properly: Either too much or too little water can be unhealthy for plant growth. Drought-stressed plants are more likely to attract spider mites.

INSPECT PLANTS FOR PESTS AND PROPERLY IDENTIFY

Learn to Identify Insects and Other Creatures: Many of them are actually beneficial and can resemble destructive pests. County Extension Agents and Master Gardeners can be helpful in identifying plant pest problems.

Avoid Treating Undiagnosed Problems. Pests attack garden plants from seed to maturity. Inspecting plants at least weekly helps you detect pest infestations early, monitor natural enemies and evaluate the effects of control tactics. Check the undersides of leaves for aphids, whiteflies and spider mites, as well as egg clusters of armyworms, Colorado potato beetles and squash bugs. To detect low populations of spider mites and thrips, beat plants on a piece of off-white paper. The pests can be seen and identified on the paper. Although yellow sticky cards are occasionally promoted as insect control devices, they are best used to monitor pest activity. These cards attract the winged adult stages of aphids, leaf miners, thrips, whiteflies and a wide variety of flies. Cards should be inspected and replaced regularly so that pests can be detected early and their numbers monitored. Sex attractant chemicals called pheromones are also available commercially to monitor many insect pests, especially moths.

CONSIDER ALL PEST SUPPRESSION METHODS

When a pest outbreak occurs, consider how it might have been prevented and the best method of reducing pest numbers to a tolerable level.

Reflective Mulches: Highly reflective mulches such as foil paper slow infestation by some pests such as aphids.

Barriers: Young plants or transplants are vulnerable to attack by cutworms, sowbugs or pillbugs. They can be protected by placing a barrier around the base of each plant. Barriers can be made of paper, cardboard, plastic or metal containers with the bottoms cut out.

Barrier Screens over the Garden: Fine mesh screens or fabric row covers can provide a barrier through which even tiny insects such as thrips cannot cross. Several products are used to cover and protect crops. When barriers are properly maintained, insects can be excluded. However, plants should still be monitored regularly, which requires removing the barrier.

Cages and trellises: Plants growing on the ground are susceptible to soil pests. Vine plants such as cucumbers and even tomatoes are easier to manage when grown in trellises or cages. It is easier to monitor pests and spray plants thoroughly when they are held up off of the ground.

High pressure water sprays: Small pests such as aphids, spider mites and others can be dislodged from plants with high pressure water sprays directed to the undersides of leaves. Commercial spray devices are available (ex: Miteyfine Sprayer www.miteyfine.com), but these devices also can be homemade. Repeated treatments may be necessary to keep pest numbers low.

Texas IPM Foundation
Integrated Pest Management or IPM.
www.tipmf.org

CONSERVE NATURAL ENEMIES AND PROTECT BEES

The first line of defense against insect pests is their natural enemies. Spiders, praying mantids, lady beetles, ground beetles, green lace wings, ambush bugs, assassin bugs, minute pirate bugs and even some wasp species prey upon insects. However, the most effective natural enemies are the tiny parasitic wasps and flies, together with bacteria, fungi and viruses that are rarely observed with the naked eye. Whether naturally occurring or released into the garden, these organisms should be preserved and encouraged to thrive. Allow natural enemies an opportunity to suppress the pest infestation. Use pesticides only as a last resort. Should a pesticide be required, select the least toxic, most target-specific pesticide that decomposes quickly in the environment.

Natural enemies can be released in the garden to control pests. Lady beetles and green lace wing larvae eat aphids and whiteflies, predaceous mites eat two-spotted spider mites and certain wasps parasitize certain insect pests. Trichogramma species develop inside caterpillar eggs and Encarsia species develop inside immature whiteflies. Companies that sell these natural enemies do not guarantee the results, particularly in outdoor sites. Factors such as the number of pests present, the environment, timing of releases, prior pesticide use and the presence of ants can affect such releases. Parasitic nematodes (Biosafe 100 and other products containing Steinernema carpocapsae) are available to control a wide variety of vegetable garden soil pests.

Bees are necessary for pollinating vegetables such as cucumbers, pumpkins, squash and melons, and should be protected. Don't apply pesticides while bees are active during the day. Instead, treat plants late in the afternoon. Avoid using products or formulations highly toxic to bees.

For more information about bees contact:
Travis County Beekeepers Association:
Email: info@traviscountybeekeepers.org
Austin Area Beekeepers Association:
www.meetup.com/Austin-Urban-Beekeeping/
Natural Enemies Handbook: *The Illustrated Guide to Biological Pest Control* by Mary Louise Flint, et al.

APPLY PESTICIDES
PROPERLY
AND ONLY
WHEN JUSTIFIED.

JULY

1	
2	
3	
4	
5	
6	
7	
8	
9	
10	
11	
12	
13	
14	
15	
16	
17	
18	
19	
20	
21	
22	
23	
24	
25	
26	
27	
28	
29	
30	
31	

/garden notes

Two of the most important things to do to keep your landscapes and gardens healthy are to use drip irrigation and apply mulch to your planting beds.

DRIP IRRIGATION

One of the best techniques to use in applying water to home landscapes, gardens and orchards is drip irrigation. This is the controlled, slow application of water to soil. The water flows under low pressure through plastic pipe or hose laid along each row of plants. The water drops out into the soil from tiny holes which are either precisely formed in the hose wall or in fittings called emitters that are plugged into the hose wall at a proper spacing. Use drip irrigation for watering vegetables, ornamental and fruit trees, shrubs, vines and container grown plants outdoors. Not recommended for lawn watering.

MULCH

A mulch is a layer of material covering the soil surface around plants. This covering benefits plants in a number of ways:
- Moderates soil temperature, thus promoting greater root development.
- Conserves moisture by reducing evaporation of water vapor from the soil surface.
- Prevents compaction by reducing soil crusting during natural rainfall or irrigation.
- Reduces disease problems.
- Keeps fruit clean while reducing rot disease by preventing soil-fruit contact.
- Reduces weed problems by 90 percent or more.

Recent research indicates that mulching does more to help newly planted trees and shrubs become established than any other factor except regular watering. Grasses and weeds, especially Bermuda grass, which grow around new plants rob them of moisture and nutrients. Mulch the entire shrub bed and mulch new trees in a 4-foot circle.

Holidays/Observances this month:
Independence Day

THINGS TO PLANT IN JULY

FLOWER PLANTS: Ageratum, Ajuga, Alpine Aster, Balsam, Blue Daze, Boltonia, Cockscomb, Silver Dollar Plant (Lunaria Annua), Periwinkle, Portulaca, Purslane, Gloriosa Daisy (Rudbeckia Hirta), Mexican Bush Sage (Salvia leucantha), Sedum, Stokes' Aster, Wax Begonia, Wishbone Flower (Torenia), Vinca, Zinnia.

FLOWER SEEDS: Ageratum, Balsam, Castor Bean, Cleome, Cockscomb, Cosmos, Four-o'clock, Gaillardia (Blanket Flower), Impatiens, Marigold, Moonflower, Morning Glory, Periwinkle, Portulaca, Tithonia, Torenia, Vinca, Zinnia.

BULBS: Autumn Crocus (Colchicum), Lirope, Lycoris, Monkey Grass.

VEGETABLES:
Early—Mid Month: Pumpkin.
Mid—Late Month: Corn, Eggplant, Peppers, Southern Pea, Tomatoes, Winter Squash.
ALL Month: Amaranth, Okra.

THINGS TO DO IN JULY

FERTILIZE: Give annuals a complete fertilizer. Water well before and after application. Deadhead and fertilize roses. Fertilize young fruit trees (except pears) with a 3-1-2 ratio product at 1-2 cups per inch of trunk diameter.

WATER: Water all planted areas deeply but infrequently during dry periods. Outdoor container plants need daily watering. Consider landscaping with drought resistant native plants in the future.

SOIL: Mulch all bare soil. Turn compost pile and add new ingredients. Clean up spring vegetable gardens and replenish with compost.

LAWN CARE: Mow every 5-7 days and leave the clippings on the lawn. Watch for take-all patch. Set mower higher in shady areas to promote denser turf.

DISEASES/PESTS TO LOOK FOR: Watch for: spider mites, leaf rollers, lacebugs and aphids on plants; chinch bugs, fleas, ticks, chiggers and grubs in lawns; scale insects on euonymus, hollies, peaches and plums; webworms in pecans and persimmons; powdery mildew on crape myrtles and roses; aphids on crape myrtle, roses and Mexican milkweed; scale on peaches and plums. Remove any diseased leaves from beds; do not add to compost.

PRUNE: Remove vigorous growth from center of peach and plum trees to prevent shading of fruiting shoots. Tip new blackberry canes at 4' to force side branches. Prune dead and damaged wood from trees and shrubs as needed.

OTHER THINGS TO DO

Plan fall gardens and prepare beds by removing perennial weeds before tilling; add compost and fertilizer. Gather herbs and flowers to dry. Preserve the bounty by freezing, canning or drying vegetables and fruits. Drink lots of water and try to stay cool.

**Need help with a Gardening Question? Call our Master Gardeners Help Desk:
512-854-9600 Monday-Friday, 9 am-5 pm
or visit our website: www.tcmastergardeners.org or email: travismg@ag.tamu.edu**

FALL VEGETABLE GARDENING TIPS by Skip Richter, Former Travis County Agrilife Extension Director

Many folks think of the South as having a long growing season. When it comes to vegetable gardening it may be more accurate to say we have two short growing seasons, spring and fall, separated by a scorching inferno called summer, not fit for man nor beast! There are a few brave edibles tough enough to bridge the gap between seasons, but they are the exceptions.

Fall vegetable gardening is in many ways better than its spring counterpart. Many vegetables such as broccoli and cauliflower seem to do best in the fall. The quality of beans, peas, root crops and many other veggies is superior when grown in the cooler days of fall. Almost anything grown in spring will do well in the fall, with the possible exception of sweet corn.

Success in fall gardening can be narrowed down to three key elements: soil, varieties and planting.

PREPARE THE SOIL PROPERLY

Soil is critical to plant growth. The importance of soil preparation cannot be over-stressed. Low organic matter, poor water holding capacity, poor drainage, low fertility and pH extremes are among the common problems with garden soil in our region. These can be at least in part alleviated through building raised beds, acidifying, fertilizing and adding organic matter during the soil preparation process.

Adding liberal amounts of composted organic matter to all types of garden soils is highly recommended. Our high pH soils in Central Texas are generally too high in calcium to be easily acidified. If your soil's pH is only in the 7.5 range, sulfur may be an option for lowering the pH adequately. All high pH soils become more forgiving when large amounts of compost are added to buffer the soil. This is largely due to the increased microbial activity that delivers the available nutrients directly to the roots.

Fertilizer may also be needed to build up the soil for the fall garden. If you have not had a soil test to tell you the nutrient content of your soil, apply 1 pound of 15-5-10 or 2 pounds of 8-2-4 and 1/2 pound of K-Mag per 100 square feet. If manures are used, 20 to 50 pounds per 100 square feet should be adequate. Thoroughly spade or till the soil to a depth of 4 to 6 inches to mix in the above ingredients.

SELECT ADAPTED VARIETIES

Here in the South we have a short season between summer heat and the first freeze in most years. Therefore it is best to select early maturing varieties (ones with short days-to-harvest intervals) to avoid having an almost-ripe bean crop lost to a freeze. If you need a copy of our Travis County Vegetable Planting Guide, which includes a list of proven varieties, call the Travis County Agrilife Extension Office: 512-854-9600.

PROPER PLANTING FOR FALL

Planting at the right time is important. We have a "window" of time in the fall when many of our warm season veggies can effectively ripen. Planting too late is setting yourself up for disappointing results.

Planting in the right way is important too. The sweltering sun creates a stressful environment for seeds and new transplants. Some gardeners have better results by starting their plants in a cool shady spot outdoors and then carefully transplanting them into the garden a few weeks later.

The most important water your crops will get is the pre-plant irrigation. If it has not rained an inch or more in the week prior to planting, give the ground a good deep soaking with a sprinkler.

Plant seeds slightly deeper (not over 3 or 4 times their width) and cover with a light mulch of hay or pine needles to give them a slightly cooler environment in which to germinate. Covering seeds with compost rather than soil will help reduce crusting and improve germination. Protect new transplants from the sun with a "lean-to" shade structure positioned on the southwest side.

New plants should be mulched about 2 inches thick to moderate soil temperatures and hold back weeds. Organic mulch such as hay, leaves, grass clippings, bark and sawdust improve water infiltration into the soil and, when plowed in at the end of the season, increase the organic matter content of the soil.

FALL PLANTING INFORMATION

VEGETABLES/DIRECT SEED
(Last Optimal Date for Maximum Yields)

Beans, snap bush	September 1
Beans, Lima Bush	August 20
Beets	October 15
Broccoli	September 1
Brussels Sprouts	September 1
Cabbage	September 1
Carrots	November 10
Cauliflower	September 1
Swiss Chard	October 15
Collards	October 10
Sweet Corn	August 20
Cucumber	September 1
Eggplant	July 20
Garlic Cloves	October 20
Kohlrabi	September 1
Lettuce (leaf)	November 10
Mustard	November 15
Onion (seed)	November 2
Parsley	October 10
Peas, southern	August 1
Pepper	July 1
Potato	September 1
Pumpkin	July 10
Radish	November 25
Spinach	November 25
Squash, Summer	September 1
Squash, Winter	July 15
Tomato	July 1
Turnip	November 1

ANNUAL FLOWERS
(Transplants Only)

Alyssum	September-December
Aster	September-December
Calendula	September-December
Chysanthemum	July-August
Dianthus	September-December
Flowering Cabbage and Kale	October-December
Pansy	October-December
Petunia	August-September
Phlox	September-December
Shasta Daisy	August-November
Snapdragon	September-November
Stock	September-December
Viola	October-December

TRANSPLANTING
(Last Optimal Date)

Tomato	July 25
Eggplant	July 25
Peppers	July 25
Broccoli	September 20
Cauliflower	September 20
Brussels Sprouts	September 20
Cabbage	September 20

VEGETABLE MATURITY RATE AND FROST SENSITIVITY

Frost-tolerant crops can withstand temperatures below 32° F.
Frost-susceptible crops are killed or injured by temperatures under 32° F.

Quick Maturing (30 to 60 days)
Frost Tolerant

Beets	Leaf Lettuce
Mustard	Radish
Spinach	Turnips

Frost Susceptible

Bush Beans	Summer Squash

Moderate Maturing (60 to 80 days)
Frost Tolerant

Broccoli	Chinese Cabbage
Carrots	Green Onions
Kohlrabi	Parsley

Frost Susceptible

Cucumber	Corn
Lima Beans	Okra
Peppers	Tomato

Slow Maturing (80 days or more)
Frost Tolerant

Brussels Sprouts	Bulb Onions
Cabbage	Cauliflower
Garlic	

Frost Susceptible

Cantaloupe	Eggplant
Irish Potato	Pumpkin
Sweet Potato	Tomato
Watermelon	Winter Squash

AUGUST

/garden notes

1	
2	
3	
4	
5	
6	
7	
8	
9	
10	
11	
12	
13	
14	
15	
16	
17	
18	
19	
20	
21	
22	
23	
24	
25	
26	
27	
28	
29	
30	
31	

Don't have a lot of space for a garden? Grow vegetables, herbs and flowers in containers.

BEST CONTAINER-GROWN VEGETABLE VARIETIES

Broccoli: Belstar, Green Magic
Cucumbers: Alibi, Little Leaf, Salad Bush, Spacemaster
Carrots: Atlas, Little Finger, Mokum
Eggplant: Fairy Tale, Gretel, Hansel, Little Fingers
Green Onions: Beltsville Bunching, Evergreen Bunching
Green Beans: Jade, Mascotte, Nickel
Lettuce: Bambi, Little Gem, Salad Bowl, Tom Thumb
Okra: Cajun Jewel, Jambalaya, Lee
Peppers: (Sweet) Ace, Cajun Belle, Camelot; (Hot) Early Jalapeno, Mariachi, Large Red Cherry
Squash: Astia, Black Beauty, Early Crookneck, Raven
Swiss Chard: Bright Lights, Magenta Sunset
Tomatoes: Husky Cherry Red, Micro Tom, Sweet Baby Girl, Better Bush, Bush Early Girl, Patio

HERBS TO GROW IN CONTAINERS

Basil-great for pestos and any tomato dishes
Bay-use fresh leaves in butters and spreads
Chives-use in butters, spreads, egg dishes, baked potatoes, soups and stews
Cilantro-traditional in salsas and pestos
Dill-leaves for many dishes, seeds for pickling
Lavender-sachets, breads, syrups and honeys
Lemon Balm-teas, breads, cookies
Mexican Mint Marigold-substitute for Tarragon
Mint-various flavors and many uses
Oregano-used in Italian and Latin foods
Parsley-pestos and dishes of all sorts
Rosemary-vegetables, teas, chicken
Sage-soups, stews and poultry stuffings
Thyme-meats, vegetables, eggs and vinegars

FLOWERS FOR CONTAINERS

Just about any bedding plant will look great. Use your imagination and create a living bouquet by grouping several containers together.

Holidays/Observances this month:
Women's Equality Day, Back to School

THINGS TO PLANT IN AUGUST

FLOWER PLANTS: Ageratum, Ajuga, Wax Begonia, Blue Daze, Boltonia, Cockscomb, Impatiens, Gloriosa Daisy (Rudbeckia Hirta), Salvia, Sedum, Shasta Daisy, Stokes' Aster, Zinnia.

FLOWER SEEDS: Ageratum, Alyssum, Amaranthus, Balsam, Bluebell, Calendula, Candytuft, Cleome, Coreopsis, Cornflower, Castor Bean, Cosmos (late), Cockscomb, Four-o'clock, Gerbera, Hollyhock, Impatiens, Linaria, Marigold (French), Moonflower, Morning Glory, Petunia, Portulaca, Sunflower, Tithonia, Flowering Tobacco, Zinnia.

BULBS: Autumn Crocus (Colchicum), Hardy Cyclamen, Louisiana Iris, Liriope, Lycoris, Monkey Grass.

VEGETABLES:
Early—Mid Month: Corn, Eggplant, Pepper, Southern Pea, Tomato, Winter Squash.
Mid—Late Month: Bush Beans, Potato.
ALL Month: Cucumber, Summer Squash.

THINGS TO DO IN AUGUST

FERTILIZE: Fertilize fruiting vegetables after first fruit set for higher productivity. Feed chrysanthemums every 2-3 weeks until buds appear, then weekly until buds show color. Fertilize roses for fall bloom. Feed berries and fruit showing poor color/vigor.

WATER: Water all planted areas deeply but infrequently during dry periods. Outdoor container plants need daily watering. Keep azaleas and fruit trees watered well because spring blooms are developing.

SOIL: Discard faded annuals and refurbish soil as needed. Prepare loose, well-drained beds for fall bulb planting. Clean up established garden beds. Turn compost pile.

LAWN CARE: Mow every 5-7 days and leave the clippings on the lawn. Set mower higher in shady areas to promote denser turf. Avoid weed killers whenever temperatures are above 85^0. Note: Avoid using weed killers containing atrazine, as this chemical leaches into our groundwater.

DISEASES/PESTS TO LOOK FOR: Watch for cutworms on new tomato transplants; protect with paper collars around base 1" above and below ground. Watch for grub worms, chinch bugs and fire ants in lawns. Check for borers in peaches, plums and other trees. Look for aphids and powdery mildew on crape myrtles.

PRUNE: Prune roses back by 1/3. Deadhead spent blooms and seed pods from crape myrtles for continued blooms. Trim photinias for red fall color. Remove dead and damaged wood from shrubs and trees. Pinch chrysanthemums for the last time.

OTHER THINGS TO DO

Try this deer repellent: spray your plants with fermented hot peppers combined with dishwashing liquid. Hot mouth for the deer!

**Need help with a Gardening Question? Call our Master Gardeners Help Desk:
512-854-9600 Monday-Friday, 9 am-5 pm
or visit our website: www.tcmastergardeners.org or email: travismg@ag.tamu.edu**

DEER-PROOFING YOUR GARDEN

What can a gardener do short of installing an eight foot fence and buying a couple of large, barking dogs? Consider planting these deer-resistant landscape plants. Just remember that in overcrowding and drought conditions, hungry deer will try to eat everything, including most of the ones on this list. (But they won't like them as much as other plants.)

LARGE TREES

All require protection with cages until they grow taller than the deer.

SMALL TREES/LARGE SHRUBS

Desert Willow (*Chilopsis linearis*)
Fig (*Ficus spp.*)
Flameleaf Sumac (*Rhus lanceolata*)
Golden Ball Lead Tree (*Leucana retusa*)
Roughleaf Dogwood (*Cornus drummondii*)
Texas Buckeye (*Aesculus agruta*)
Texas Persimmon (*Diospyros texana*)
Texas Mountain Laurel (*Sophora secundiflora*)

SHRUBS

Abelia (*Abelia spp.*)
Acuba (*Acuba japonica*)
Agarita (*Berberis trifoliata*)
Autumn Aster (*Aster spp.*)
Autumn Sage (*Salvia greggii*)
Blackberry (*Rubus spp.*) (Thorny variety only)
Boxwood (*Buxus microphylla*)
Cenizo/Texas Sage (*Leucophyllum spp.*)
Cotoneaster (Coral Beauty) (*Cotoneaster dammeri*)
Dwarf Chinese Holly (*Ilex cornuta*)
Dwarf Yaupon (*Ilex vomitoria*)
Elaegnus (*Elaegnus spp.*)
Evergreen sumac (*Rhus virens*)
Fragrant Mimosa (*Mimosa borealis*)
Japanese Aralia (*Aralia sieboldii*)
Jerusalem Cherry (*Solanum pseudocapsicum*)
Juniper (*Juniperus spp.*)
Lantana (*Lantana urticoides*) (Natives only)
Mexican Buckeye (*Ungnadia speciosa*)
Mexican Oregano (*Poliomintha longifolia*)
Mexican Silktassle (*Garrya lindheimeri*)
Nandina (*Nandina spp.*)
Oleander (*Nerium oleander*)
Pampas Grass (*Cortaderia spp.*)
Pyracantha (*Pyracantha coccinea*)
Red-leaf or Japanese Barberry (*Berberis thunbergii*)
Rosemary (*Rosemarinus officinalis*)
Scotch Broom (*Cytisus scoparius*)
Turk's Cap (*Malvaviscus arboreus*)
Wax Myrtle (*Myrica cerifera*)

PERENNIAL SUCCULENTS AND LILIES

Cactus (*Opuntia spp.*) (Any with stout spines)
Cast Iron Plant (*Aspidistra lurida*)
Hen and Chicks (*Sempervivum spp.*) (Spiny varieties)
Lily-of-the-Nile (*Agapanthus spp.*)
Red Yucca (*Hesperaloe parviflora*) (flowers will be eaten)
Sacahuista/Bear Grass/Nolina (*Nolina spp.*)
Sotol (*Dasylirion spp.*)
Yucca (*Yucca spp.*)

VINES

Carolina Jessamine (*Gelsemium sempervirens*)
Star Jasmine (*Trachelospermum jasminoides*)

GROUND COVERS

Aarons Beard (*Hypericum calycinum*)
Asiatic Jasmine (*Trachelospermum asiaticum*)
Carpet Bugle (*Ajuga reptans*)
Monkey Grass (*Ophiopogon japonica*)
Myrtle (*Vinca Major*)
Santolina (*Santolina spp.*)
Spearmint (*Menta spicata*)

FLOWERS, FERNS, HERBS

Ageratum (*Ageratum spp.*)
Begonia (*Begonia spp.*)
Black-eyed Susan (*Rudbeckia hirta*)
Blackfoot Daisy (*Melampodium leucanthum*)
Bluebonnet (*Lupinus texensis*)
Cedar Sage (*Salvia roemeriana*)
Chrysanthemum (*Chrysanthemum spp.*) (Flowers will be eaten)
Coreopsis (*Coreopsis spp.*)
Cosmos (*Cosmos bipinnatus*)
Dusty Miller (*Senecio cineraria*)
Flame Acanthus (*Aniscanthus wrightii*)
Foxglove (*Digitalis spp.*)
Indigo Spires (*Salvia x 'Indigo Spires'*)
Iris (*Iris spp.*)
Mealy Blue Sage (*Salvia farinacea*)
Mexican Bush Sage (*Salvia leucantha*)
Mexican Mint Marigold (*Tagetes spp.*)
Periwinkle (*Vinca rosea*)
Purple Cone Flower (*Echinacea angustifolia*)
Sword Fern (*Nephrolepis*)
Verbena (*Verbena spp.*)
Wood Fern (*Dryopteris spp.*)
Yarrow (*Achillea filipendulina*)
Zexmenia (*Zexmenia hispida*)
Zinnia (*Zinnia spp.*)

Deer-Proofing Your Yard & Garden by Rhonda Massingham Hart, Gwen Steege
Gardening in Deer Country by Vincent Jr. Drzewucki, et al.

Plants are considered diseased when they do not grow and develop normally. The cause of such a condition may result from infection by disease-causing organisms or from environmental factors. Organisms known to cause disease are bacteria, fungi, nematodes, viruses, mycoplasmas and parasitic seed plants. Examples of environmental disorders are air pollution, poor soil, excessive heat, low or excessive nutrition, and drought.

When organisms cause disease, it is usually due to a parasitic relationship with a host plant. The parasite, or causal organism, is called a pathogen. The interaction between host and pathogen results in disease.

Prevention is the best approach to plant disease control when using either chemical or non-chemical (organic) methods. Prevention may involve suppressing the disease agent or avoiding the disease. Utilizing as many disease-preventative practices as possible will ensure the best possible control.

SUPPRESS THE DISEASE AGENT

Rotation: Vegetables in the same family group are more likely to be susceptible to the same soil-borne diseases. Cantaloupes and watermelons, for example, have common diseases. If they follow each other in a rotation, a disease organism may be limited on the first crop but sustain enough carry-over in the soil to cause severe loss on the following crop. Vegetables from different family groups should follow each other in a rotation because they are usually not susceptible to the same disease organisms. *See page 18 for information about rotation of crops.*

Organic Matter: Organic matter increases the number and kind of microorganisms in the soil. Many of these microorganisms compete with disease agents for nourishment. In most cases, the best organic matter is obtained by turning under a green cover crop, such as a small grain (wheat, oats, barley, cereal rye) or a legume. Compost can also be tilled into the soil.

Resistant Varieties: Resistance may mean a plant does not get a particular disease. It could also be expressed as slower disease development which allows resistant plants to produce an acceptable yield before or without losing vigor to disease attack.

Sanitation: Any crop residue destruction practice that reduces the disease agent's ability to reproduce or overseason could be included under sanitation. In most cases, it is best not to put diseased plant parts in a compost pile. Diseased plant tissue should be buried, burned, or disposed of in some other way.

Fallowing: Leaving land idle and clean after the growing season will reduce disease agents in the soil. Fallowing is especially helpful if done in the summer months when soil temperatures are high.

Weed Control: Weeds harbor insects and serve as hosts for many virus diseases. For most viruses to survive, they must remain in a living organism whether it is a host plant or insect. Destroying weeds in and around the garden may eliminate potential overwintering host plants.

AVOID DISEASE

Change Planting Date: Some diseases can be controlled by changing the planting date. Spring-planted squash usually escapes mosaic virus, whereas fall-planted squash does not. Warm-season vegetables, like peas and okra, should be planted after soils warm sufficiently to avoid seedling disease.

Obtain Disease-Free Planting Stock: It is advisable to check transplants such as tomatoes, peppers and others for root knot nematode galls. Certified Irish seed potatoes are less likely than uncertified potatoes to harbor a disease such as black leg. Some disease agents are seed transmitted; thus, only the best seed should be planted.

Cultural Practices: Select the best site. Choose a site with deep, well drained soil.

Plant on raised beds. Raised beds improve drainage. They also warm up faster than level soil, which aids in faster emergence. Slow emergence increases chances of seedling disease.

Use proper plant spacing. Crowded plants reduce air circulation which enhances leaf spot diseases. Septoria leaf spot on tomatoes is an example.

Overplant: Overplanting (e.g., 12 tomato plants instead of 6) will ensure enough production in case plants or fruit are lost to disease.

Proper Fertilization: Plants receiving all needed nutrients may resist some disease-causing organisms.

Do Not Overwater: Excessively wet conditions increase soil-borne fungal diseases like root rots and wilts.

Avoid overhead irrigation. Leaf spot diseases develop rapidly when leaves are moist.

Do Not Prune Roots: Roots cut while cultivating reduce plant vigor and leave openings for root rot and wilt fungi to enter.

For more information:
512-974-2581 or www.austintexas.gov/department/grow-green

SEPTEMBER

1	
2	
3	
4	
5	
6	
7	
8	
9	
10	
11	
12	
13	
14	
15	
16	
17	
18	
19	
20	
21	
22	
23	
24	
25	
26	
27	
28	
29	
30	

/garden notes

There's still time to plant a fall garden this month and harvest before the first freeze. See information on page 47 for details.

TIME TO DIVIDE PERENNIALS

September is the perfect time to divide and transplant daylilies, bearded iris, Shasta daisies, violets, wood ferns and cannas. Share extras with friends and neighbors.

Time to groom and tidy up pot plants that have been outside in preparation for bringing inside before the first freeze. Check for insect problems and fertilize before bringing inside.

OVERUSED SHRUBS--AVOID PLANTING

Red Tip Photinia: When planted as a shrub, requires constant pruning to prevent it growing into a small tree. Subject to fungal spot and cotton root rot. **(Avoid planting: invasive)**
Nandina (Avoid planting: invasive)
Pittosporum Subject to freezing.
Euonymus (variegated) Subject to scale, color reversion and short lived.
Ligustrum Subject to scale, grows to a small tree unless pruned diligently. **(Avoid planting: invasive)**

SOME RECOMMENDED SHRUBS

Abelia	Burford Holly
Acuba	Cotoneaster
Agarita	Rosemary
Barberry	Sago Palm
Beautyberry	Yaupon Holly

See list on page 12 for more suggestions. Plant native and adapted species for less maintenance.

Holidays/Observances this month:
Labor Day, Grandparent's Day, Citizenship Day, Autumnal Equinox (Fall Begins)

THINGS TO PLANT IN SEPTEMBER

FLOWER PLANTS: Ajuga, Alpine Aster, Wax Begonia, Boltonia, Butterfly Weed, Calico Plant, Candytuft, Chinese Forget-Me-Not (Cynoglossum amabile), Cockscomb, Cornflower, Dianthus, Daisy (English, Shasta and Painted), Euryops, Impatiens, Larkspur, Liatris, Lobelia, Petunia, Phlox (divaricata and paniculata), Obedient Plant (Physostegia), Salvia (perennial types), Sedum, Stock, Stokes' Aster.

FLOWER SEEDS: Alyssum, African Daisy (Arctotis), Balsam, Bluebell, Bluebonnet, Calendula, Castor Bean, Cockscomb, Columbine, Cornflower, Cosmos, Daisy, Delphinium, Four-o'clock, Hollyhock, Larkspur, Liatris, Marigold (French), Poppy, Snapdragon, Stock, Sunflower.

BULBS: Allium, Amarcrinum, Calla, Autumn Crocus (Colchicum), Cooperia, Daylily, Dietes, Hardy Cyclamen, Spider Lily (Hymerocallis), Liriope, Louisiana Iris, Ipheion, Lily, Lycoris, Oxalis, Monkey Grass, Rain Lily, Scilla, Watsonia. Purchase Tulip, Crocus, Hyacinth and Daffodil bulbs to pre-chill.

VEGETABLES:
Early—Mid Month: Beans, Summer Squash.
Mid—Late Month: Broccoli, Cabbage, Cauliflower, Chinese Cabbage, Collards, Garlic, Kohlrabi, Peas (English & edible pod).

FRUIT: Strawberries. Prepare soil now for winter fruit tree planting.

THINGS TO DO IN SEPTEMBER

FERTILIZE: Feed chrysanthemums every 2-3 weeks until buds appear, then weekly until buds show color. Fertilize roses, gardenias and magnolias.

WATER: Water trees and shrubs deeply and slowly.

DIVIDE: Transplant after dividing: Amaryllises, Callas, Cannas, Daylilies, Irises, Liriope, Wood Ferns.

SOIL: Test soil every three years to help plan fertilizer applications. Start a compost pile with fall leaves and yard debris; shred with lawnmower. Replenish mulch in beds.

LAWN CARE: Watch for brown patch in St. Augustine turf as temperatures cool. Lawns with a history of the disease should be sprayed in late month and again in three weeks with Terraclor or Daconil. Early morning is the best time to water lawns. Mow every 5-7 days, leaving the clippings on the lawn.

DISEASES/PESTS TO LOOK FOR: Watch roses for blackspot and mildew. Fall webworms are easiest to control when treated early with Bacillus thuringiensis (Bt).

PRUNE: Remove dead and damaged wood from shrubs and trees. Lightly prune pyracanthas so berries will show.

OTHER THINGS TO DO

Trick Poinsettias into holiday bloom. Beginning on the fall equinox (September 21/22) make sure potted plants get 14 hours of darkness every 24 hour period. Use a water-soluble fertilizer mixed about 1/4 strength with every watering. Plants should show color around Thanksgiving. At that point, restore them to bright, indirect sunlight and cut back on fertilizer.

**Need help with a Gardening Question? Call our Master Gardeners Help Desk:
512-854-9600 Monday-Friday, 9 am-5 pm
or visit our website: www.tcmastergardeners.org or email: travismg@ag.tamu.edu**

RECOMMENDED WILDFLOWER VARIETIES

Black-eyed Susan
(Rudbeckia hirta)
Perennial/full sun.
Excellent cut flower.

Blanket Flower
(G. aristata)
Perennial/full sun. Keep cut back for continual bloom.

Bluebonnet
(Lupinus texensis, L. Subcarnosus)
Annual/full sun. Purchase scarified seed or soak for 3-4 days in warm water to soften seed coat.

Butterfly Weed
(Asclepias tuberosa)
Perennial/full sun. Attracts butterflies; plants disappear during dormant season.

Clasping Coneflower
(Rudbeckia amplexicaulis)
Annual/full sun.
Excellent cut flower; prefers moist soil.

Crimson Clover
(Trifolium incarnatum)
Annual/full sun.
Plant by itself, as it will crowd out other flowers.

Drummond Phlox
(Phlox drummondii)
Annual/full sun.
Fragrant blooms; loves sandy soil with good drainage.

Firewheel, Indian Blanket
(Gaillardia pulchella)
Annual/full sun. Keep cut back for continual bloom.

Gay Feather
(Liatris micronata)
Perennial/full sun, partial shade.
Excellent cut flower; suitable for drying; takes two years to bloom.

Lemon mint
(Monarda citriodora)
Annual/full sun. Attracts bees, butterflies and hummingbirds; seedpods great for dried flower arrangement.

Mealy Blue Sage
(Salvia farinaceae)
Perennial/full sun, partial shade.
From seed, cuttings; long spikes of deep blue flowers.

Mexican Hat
(Ratibida columnaris)
Perennial/full sun. Excellent cut flower; reseeds freely.

Moss Verbena
(Verbena tenuisecta)
Perennial/full sun.
Drought tolerant; low spreading plant.

Plains Coreopsis
(C. tinctoria)
Annual/full sun. Very tolerant of wet or dry areas; dwarf red form available.

Purple Coneflower
(Echinacea purpurea)
Perennial/full sun. Excellent cut flower.

Scarlet Sage
(Salvia coccinea)
Perennial/full sun, partial shade.
Attracts hummingbirds and butterflies; cut back in summer to keep compact.

Showy Primrose
(Oenothera speciosa)
Perennial/full sun.
Takes 2 years to bloom.

Texas Paintbrush
(Castelleja indivisa)
Annual/full sun.
Grows best with native grasses.

Tick-seed, Lance-leaved Coreopsis
(Coreopsis lancelota)
Perennial/sun. Start from seed, division, cuttings.

For additional information:

Databases of Texas Plants
www.wildflower.org/plants
www.plants.usda.gov/checklist

Lady Bird Johnson Wildflower Center
4801 LaCross Ave., Austin, TX 78739
512-232-0100 www.wildflower.org

Native Plant Society of Texas
State Organization: www.npsot.org/
Austin Chapter: www.npsot.org/Austin/

LARGE TREES

Bald Cypress
Bigtooth Maple
Bur Oak
Cedar Elm
Chinquapin Oak
Live Oak
Texas Red Oak
Pecan
Shumard Oak
Southern Live Oak
Southern Magnolia
Texas Walnut

SMALL TREES AND SHRUBS

Agarita
American Beautyberry
Deciduous Holly
Desert Willow
Dwarf Yaupon Holly
Evergreen Sumac
Flame Acanthus
Flame Leaf Sumac
Kidneywood
Mexican Buckeye
Mexican Plum
Nolina/Sacahuista
Prickly Pear
Red Buckeye
Redbud
Rusty Blackhaw Viburnum
Sotol
Texas Mountain Laurel
Texas Sage (Cenizo)
Wood Fern
Yaupon Holly
Yucca

VINES

Carolina Yellow Jessamine
Crossvine
Coral Honeysuckle
Passion Flower
Trumpet Vine
Virginia Creeper

For more information: *Native Texas Gardens: Maximum Beauty, Minimum Upkeep* and *Native Texas Plants: Landscaping Region by Region* by Sally Wasowski, Andy Wasowski

WHY SHOULD I USE NATIVE PLANTS?

Native plants provide a beautiful, hardy, drought resistant, low maintenance landscape while benefiting the environment. Native plants, once established, save time and money by eliminating or significantly reducing the need for fertilizers, pesticides, water and lawn maintenance equipment.

Native plants do not require fertilizers. Vast amounts of fertilizers are applied to lawns. Excess phosphorus and nitrogen (the primary components of most fertilizers) run off into lakes and rivers causing excess algae growth. This depletes oxygen in our waters, harms aquatic life and interferes with recreational uses.

Native plants require fewer pesticides than lawns. Nationally, over 70 million pounds of pesticides are applied to lawns each year. Pesticides run off lawns and can contaminate rivers and lakes. People and pets in contact with chemically treated lawns can be harmed.

Native plants require less water than lawns. The modern lawn requires significant amounts of water to thrive. In urban areas, lawn irrigation uses as much as 30% of the water consumption on the East Coast and up to 60% on the West Coast. The deep root systems of many native plants increase the soil's capacity to store water. Native plants can significantly reduce water runoff and, consequently, flooding.

Native plants help reduce air pollution. Natural landscapes do not require mowing. Lawns, however, must be mowed regularly. Gas-powered garden tools emit 5% of the nation's air pollution. Forty million lawn mowers consume 200 million gallons of gasoline per year. One gas-powered lawn mower emits 11 times the air pollution of a new car for each hour of operation.

Native plants provide shelter and food for wildlife. Native plants attract a variety of birds, butterflies and other wildlife by providing diverse habitats and food sources. Closely mowed lawns are of little use to most wildlife.

Native plants promote biodiversity and stewardship of our natural heritage. In the U.S., approximately 20 million acres of lawn are cultivated, covering more land than any single crop. Native plants are a part of our natural heritage. Natural landscaping is an opportunity to reestablish diverse native plants, thereby inviting the birds and butterflies back home.

**For additional information:
Native Plant Society**
www.npsot.org/

OCTOBER

1	
2	
3	
4	
5	
6	
7	
8	
9	
10	
11	
12	
13	
14	
15	
16	
17	
18	
19	
20	
21	
22	
23	
24	
25	
26	
27	
28	
29	
30	
31	

/garden notes

Now is the best time to plant new trees and shrubs. The planting hole should be only as deep as the root ball and 2 to 3 times wider. No need to amend the soil or add fertilizer at planting time. Return the original soil, firm and water well. Mulch 3-4 inches deep around plant, avoiding the trunk.

Fertilize established trees and shrubs to maintain growth and health during the coming winter weather stresses. Water well. Replenish mulch.

FALL PLANTED, SPRING FLOWERING ANNUALS

Calendula-Attractive cut flowers.

California Poppy-Attractive cut flowers, can be direct seeded.

Dianthus-Single carnation, bright colors, hardy.

Flowering Kale-Ornamental foliage, very hardy, edible.

Flowering Cabbage-Ornamental foliage, very hardy, edible.

Iceland Poppy-Attractive cut flowers, can be direct seeded.

Larkspur-Good for masses of color.

Nasturtium-Do not over fertilize, needs good drainage.

Pansy-Hardy, wide color range.

Snapdragon-Many varieties and colors.

Stock-Spike flowers.

Sweet Peas-Fragrant, good cut flowers.

Viola-Excellent small flowered annual.

OTHER THINGS TO DO

Move tropicals inside before temperatures fall below 50^0 F. Be prepared for an early freeze. Pre-chill tulip, crocus, late-flowering daffodil and hyacinth bulbs in the refrigerator.

Holidays/Observances this month:
Columbus Day, Halloween

THINGS TO PLANT IN OCTOBER

FLOWER PLANTS: Ajuga, Alyssum, Bluebonnet, Butterfly Weed, Calendula, Candytuft, Carnation, Chinese Forget-Me-Not (Cynoglossum amabile), Clarkia (Godetia), Cornflower, Dianthus, Daisy (English and Painted), Euryops, Forget-Me-Not (Myositis), Gazania, Indian Blanket, Liatris, Nasturtium, Pansy, Penstemon, Petunia, Phlox (divaricata and paniculata), Obedient Plant (Physostegia), German Primrose (Primula obconica), Salvia farinacea, Sedum, Snapdragon, Stock.

FLOWER SEEDS: Alyssum, African Daisy (Arctotis), Bluebonnet, Calendula, Columbine, Coreopsis, Cornflower, Daisy, Delphinium, Hollyhock, Larkspur, Nasturtium, Pansy, Petunia, Phlox, Pinks, California Poppy, Scabiosa, Snapdragon, Stock, Sweet Pea, Viola, Wildflowers.

BULBS: Allium, Amarcrinum, Calla, Autumn Crocus (Colchicum), Cooperia, Daylily, Dietes, Hardy Cyclamen, Spider Lily (Hymerocallis), Liriope, Louisiana Iris, Ipheion, Lily, Lycoris, Oxalis, Monkey Grass, Rain Lily, Scilla, Watsonia. Purchase Tulip, Crocus, Daffodil and Hyacinth bulbs for chilling.

VEGETABLES:
Early—Mid Month: Arugula, Broccoli, Cabbage, Cauliflower, Chinese Cabbage, Kohlrabi.
Mid—Late Month: Carrot, Endive, Lettuce, Spinach, Turnip.
All Month: Beets, Chard, Collards, Garlic, Kale, Mustard, Multiplier Onion, Radish.
Dig sweet potatoes before first frost.

HERBS: Borage, Burnet, Caraway, Catnip, Celeriac, Chamomile, Chervil, Chives, Comfrey, Cilantro, Cumin, Dill, Fennel, Fenugreek, Lemon Balm, Mexican Mint Marigold, Mint, Oregano, Parsley, Rosemary, Sage, Santolina, Winter Savory, Sorrel, Thyme, Yarrow.

FRUIT: Strawberries.

THINGS TO DO IN OCTOBER

FERTILIZE: Fertilize existing beds of iris with well-rotted manure or balanced fertilizer. Reduce houseplant fertilizer by 1/2 for winter.

WATER: Water areas as needed.

TRANSPLANT: Divide and transplant crowded perennials. Dig and store caladium bulbs. Dust with fungicide.

PREPARE SOIL: Mulch gingers and other tropicals that overwinter outdoors to retain warmth and moisture and to control weeds. Falling leaves make autumn a good time to start a compost pile. Shred (or mow) leaves to speed decomposition. Turn compost pile periodically and keep it moist.

LAWN CARE: Fertilize with 3-1-2 ratio fertilizer. In newly-plugged lawns, sow 8 lbs. of ryegrass per 1,000 sq. ft. to help hold soil. The seed grass will make a bright green carpet until spring, when hot weather will kill rye. Not recommended for established lawns. Mow every 5-7 days and leave the clippings on the lawn.

DISEASES/PESTS TO LOOK FOR: Check for cabbage loopers in the garden; spray with Bacillus thuringiensis (Bt). Make second treatment for brown patch on lawns with a history of the disease.

PRUNE: Prune shrubs as needed, but save major pruning for the winter. Remove dead and damaged wood from shrubs and trees. Make cuttings of tender plants before frost.

BASIL/Annual: Sweet Basil most common, easy to grow. Large glossy green leaves. Anise flavored. Great for pestos. The most popular and a favorite of all good cooks. A must for good basil vinegars. Used primarily in seasoning spaghetti sauces, stews, soups and many other dishes. Also **Lemon.**

Purple Ruffles easy to grow, not used much in cooking, however, great for adding a couple of leaves to the sweet basil in making vinegars, to give it a champagne pink color.

Cinnamon excellent in cookies, cakes, and another one to add to arrangements, green or dried for adding aroma. A favorite.

Spicy Globe small globe shaped ornamental type. Culinary.

BAY LAUREL/Perennial: A marvelous plant that can be grown in a large container. It can freeze, particularly during the extreme low wind chill days. Plant in a large pot, easy to bring inside during the winter. Fresh bay leaves are excellent when used in butters and spreads.

BORAGE/Annual: May grow to three feet tall. Its leaves are gray-green and it produces bright blue star-shape flowers. Seed it in the garden because it is difficult to transplant. It grows best in full sun but does fairly well in partial shade. This herb is grown for its leaves which should be harvested before the plant flowers.

CATNIP/Perennial: Makes a soothing and sleep-inducing tea. Can be sewn in sachets or pillows to create a "sleep pillow." Cats love it. They will wallow in the bed where it grows. If a problem, plant some in a hanging basket.

CHIVES/Perennial: Onion used in many dishes-such as spreads, butters, baked potatoes, soups, stews and more. The flowers are lavender, used in salads. Chives can be blended in water and used as an insect repellent or grown among plants that may harbor unpleasant insects. Chives, garlic, onions and leeks make excellent repellents.

Garlic has a delicate garlic flavor-when dried will not hold its flavor as well as the onion chive, but is great as a fresh addition to foods. Its flower is white and also can be eaten, added to salads. Flowers of both chives can be floated on punch bowls. When trimming chives, cut them about 1/2 inch from the ground. They will then produce new growth. They need to be propagated by root division in about three years. A must in every garden.

CILANTRO/CORIANDER/Annual: Also known as Chinese parsley, used in salsa, can be blended into a pesto. It likes full sun, but does not like the summer heat, which causes it to bolt quickly and go to seed. Coriander is a spice made from the ripened seeds of the cilantro plant.

DILL/Annual: Dillweed (the leaves) is a favorite for many dishes. The seeds are used in pickling and vinegars. A cool weather plant. Harvest the outside leaves. Best seeded directly into the soil to prevent early bolting.

EPAZOTE /Annual: Famous for eliminating the embarrassing consequences of eating beans. Add to food 15 minutes before serving. It thrives in dry soil and will reseed. Use in salsas, corn and squash dishes and poultry sauces.

FENNEL/Annual: Bronze beautiful in the garden due to the outstanding color. Great in soups, fish or chopped in salads. Grows to four feet.

Florence often grown for its seed or bulbs. Grows to 3' tall in full sun with lots of water. The yellow flowers can be dried for arrangements.

GARLIC/Annual: Silver Skin small bulbs are excellent in cooking, also considered an excellent source for health reasons. An annual which must be planted in September-October and will mature in the months of June-July in our area. Excellent for all types of dishes.

SCENTED GERANIUMS/Perennial: (needs winter protection). Lemon Rose, Peppermint, Snowflake, Peach, Apple, Cinnamon, Ginger, Lemon-Lime, Lime, Chocolate and many others. Are used as an addition to cookies, cakes, teas and other desserts, in addition to being used in oils, vinegars and potpourris.

LAVENDER/Perennial: English grows to two feet, is bushy, full and seems easier to grow than the French. Cannot tolerate extreme heat, so protect roots with a pea gravel mulch. Used in perfumes, sachets, all types of cosmetics, and can be used for making breads, syrups and honeys. Rub on insect bites to ease pain and promote healing. Water infrequently (about every 7-10 days) without wetting the leaves which will prevent the growth of a plant-killing fungus.

LEMON BALM/Perennial: A hardy perennial in our area, can be invasive. It can be considered a friendship plant, as it has so many qualities and uses, anyone would be happy to have a starter plant. It can be propagated from the separation of root system as well. It makes a wonderful tea, is used in many dishes such as breads and cookies.

LEMON GRASS/Perennial: (must be winter protected). A relative of the Pampas Grass, grows to four feet. The strongest lemon flavor is in the lower end of the stem (small bulb) section. Makes a great tea, also a substitute for lemon in foods such as sauces. Harvest the stem right down to the ground level and chop like a scallion. Grows from full sun to part shade. Produces the lemon oil that is used in many household products as well. The tops will burn during a freeze, the entire plant needs to be mulched and protected from freezes.

LEMON VERBENA/Perennial: The strongest of the lemon herbs, with beautiful lavender flowers. Does best when cut back to control sprawly growth. Is excellent used in teas, dried for later uses in teas, cakes and cookies. Protect from bitter cold winters.

MARJORAM/Annual: (can winter over in greenhouse). Sweet or mild oregano, every cook needs one in their herb bed or window box. Used in many meat and vegetable dishes. Grows from 6-9 inches. Needs full sun and moderate water.

MINT/Perennial: Apple, Chocolate, Corsican, English, Lemon-Lime, Lime, Orange, Peppermint, Pineapple, Spearmint, and Wintergreen, to name a few. There are many types of mints and many uses. It is invasive, but can be contained by planting in large pots or encircling the desired area with a metal trim placed in the ground, below the root system depth. Likes moist soil and will grow well in sun or shade. Keep the plant well trimmed.

OREGANO/Perennial: Italian related to Marjoram but stronger, used in many dishes such as Italian and Latin foods. A must. A perennial that needs some protection in winter.

Mexican used in the same manner as all other oreganos, especially in Latin foods. A nice plant to put in a large pot, protect from extreme heat and cold. Hummingbirds love the flowers.

PARSLEY/Biennial: Italian large flat leaf. Great for chopping for making pestos and dishes of all sorts. Used in many foods, salads, spreads, butters, meats and vegetables.

Curly Leaf a beautiful plant in the herb garden, very hardy, wonderful in dishes. All Parsleys are biennials, some get very large. Use the very bottom leaves first for cooking. Parsley is a great source of iron, magnesium, and iodine. You can grow both kinds in full sun to part shade.

PENNYROYAL/Perennial: An excellent flea and mosquito repellent, this is a strong smelling mint, and easily grown as a ground cover. Makes an excellent hanging basket or pot herb, but needs the rootball trimmed back and new soil added several times a year. Planted around pet quarters will repel fleas.

ROSEMARY/Perennial: There are many Rosemarys. **Prostrate** is a low growing, sprawling plant reaching 2-3 ft. in height. Rosemary grows well in the ground in our area. If a freeze threatens, cover the plants with blankets.

The **Upright** types can get quite large-up to 6-8 ft. Some of the uprights are more cold hardy, such as the Arp. All need some winter protection and do well if planted in an enclosure and protected. Used in many vegetable dishes, teas and baked goods, also excellent on baked chicken.

SAGE/Perennial: Garden Sage one of the Mediterranean herbs that does not like to be in soggy soil. Best to let dry out before watering. Key ingredient in soups, stews and poultry stuffings. If you ever use the fresh, you won't want to go back to the ground store bought type.

Pineapple a favorite for appearance and flavor. Grows to 4 ft., has lush green leaves and red flowers that are attractive to hummingbirds and butterflies. Use the leaves in teas and in baked goods. The flowers are pretty in punch bowls.

Tricolor variegated leaves of white, purple and green. Use as garden sage.

SALAD BURNET/Perennial: Grows in a rosette clump with rounded serrated leaves having a mild cucumber taste. Likes fairly dry limestone soil and full sun. Attractive as a border plant. Use in sandwiches, herb vinegars and salads or sprinkle over fish.

SORREL/Perennial: A hardy perennial growing to 18" tall in full sun with shade in the afternoon. A great salad herb, has a lemony flavor when using the young leaves raw. The older leaves can be cooked as greens or used to wrap baked fish. Makes a wonderful, tart soup.

TARRAGON/Perennial: Mexican Mint Marigold grown as a substitute for true tarragon. Will survive our winters if heavily mulched or covered during extreme cold times. Has an anise scent and can be used in many dishes and vinegars. Has small marigold flowers in the fall.

TRUE TARRAGON does not do well in our humid climate.

THYME/Perennial: Comes in several different types. Common thyme is grown in most gardens. It is a perennial which produces a shrub-like plant about one foot tall. It produces purple flowers and gray-green leaves. Use the leaves in stews, with most beef, lamb, pork and chicken dishes. Great with fish, leafy vegetables and beans.

For additional information:
Austin Herb Society
www.austinherbsociety.org/

Books about Herbs:
Herbs for Texas
by Howard Garrett, Odena Brannam

Rodale's Successful Organic Gardening: Herbs
by Patricia S. Michalak

The Herb Garden Cookbook: The Complete Gardening and Gourmet Guide by Lucinda Hutson, Cooke Photographics, Melody Lambert

Special thanks to Vee Fowler of the Austin Herb Society for contributing her expertise to this article.

NOVEMBER

1	
2	
3	
4	
5	
6	
7	
8	
9	
10	
11	
12	
13	
14	
15	
16	
17	
18	
19	
20	
21	
22	
23	
24	
25	
26	
27	
28	
29	
30	

/garden notes

Bring a bit of spring cheer to winter's gloomy days by 'forcing' Paperwhites and Amaryllis into bloom inside the home. Simply put into a pot or vase and keep watered (soil not required nor is chilling).

OTHER THINGS TO DO

Tulips, crocus and late flowering daffodil bulbs need at least six weeks of pre-chilling in the refrigerator (with no vegetables or fruits in the same section to give off gasses that will kill the flower bud). Best to plant by late November.

The best bulbs for our area include wild and lily-flowered tulips, jonquils, very early daffodils, muscari, leucojum and squills (Neglectum species). Plant bulbs at depths recommended in chart, below.

Time to get the garden ready for the new growing season. Clean, repair and replace garden tools. Create a garden plan to organize your chores and planting schedules.

FALL PLANTED BULBS
(Recommended Planting Depth)

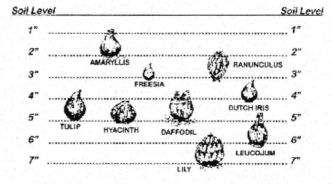

(Advice on bulbs for Austin provided by Judy Osburn, Master Gardener)

Holidays/Observances this month:
Daylight Saving Time ends (1st Sunday), Election Day, Veterans Day, Average First Freeze, Thanksgiving Day

THINGS TO PLANT IN NOVEMBER

FLOWER PLANTS: Ajuga, Alyssum, Bluebonnet, Butterfly Weed, Calendula, Candytuft, Carnation, Chinese Forget-Me-Not (Cynoglossum amabile), Cornflower, Dianthus, Daisy (African, English and Painted), Euryops, Forget-Me-Not (Myositis), Gazania, Indian Blanket, Liatris, Nasturtium, Ornamental Cabbage and Kale, Pansy, Penstemon, Petunia, Phlox paniculata, Obedient Plant (Physostegia), German Primrose (Primula obconica), Snapdragon, Stock.

FLOWER SEEDS: Alyssum, Bluebonnet, Calendula, Candytuft, Cornflower, Daisy, Delphinium, Hollyhock, Larkspur, Nasturtium, Pansy, Petunia, Phlox, Pinks, California Poppy, Scabiosa, Snapdragon, Sweet Pea, Sweet William, Verbena, Viola, Wildflowers.

BULBS: Agapanthus, Allium, Alstroemeria, Amarcrinum, Amaryllis (in container), Anemone, Ground Orchid (Bletilla), Calla, Crinum, Crocus, Daffodil, Freesia, Spider Lily (Hymerocallis), Ipheion, Dutch Iris, Spuria Iris, Ixia, Snowflake (Leucojum), Lily, Liriope, Monkey Grass, Muscari, Star of Bethlehem (Orthinogalum), Rain Lily, Society Garlic, Spraxis, Aztec Lily (Sprekelia), Watsonia.

VEGETABLES:
Early—Mid Month: Carrot, Chard, Mustard, Turnip.
All Month: Kale, Lettuce, Radish, Spinach.

HERBS: Borage, Burnet, Caraway, Catnip, Celeriac, Chamomile, Chervil, Chives, Comfrey, Cilantro, Cumin, Dill, Fennel, Fenugreek, Lemon Balm, Mexican Mint Marigold, Mint, Oregano, Parsley, Rosemary, Sage, Santolina, Winter Savory, Sorrel, Thyme, Yarrow.

FRUIT: Strawberries.

THINGS TO DO IN NOVEMBER

FERTILIZE: Fertilize strawberry beds with a 3-1-2 ratio fertilizer. Keep soil moist to promote good plant vigor and berry production next spring.

WATER: Water everything well before a freeze, but avoid overwatering.

TRANSPLANT: Divide and replant crowded perennials throughout the winter months. Transplant chives, garlic and multiplying onions. Now is the best time to move woody ornamentals. Prepare the new site before transplanting.

PREPARE SOIL: Have landscape and garden soils tested now to determine soil balancing needs. Forms are available at the Extension Office, 1600-B Smith Road, Austin, TX, 78721 or call 512-854-9600. Check winter mulch and replenish if needed. Stockpile leaves for mulch and composting throughout spring and summer.

LAWN CARE: Bring a sample of problem turf into the Travis County Agrilife Extension Office in a labeled plastic bag for analysis. A mulching mower makes raking leaves obsolete or use grass catcher as a mulch catcher. Use shredded leaves and grass clippings as a mulch or put into the compost bin.

DISEASES/PESTS TO LOOK FOR: Watch roots of removed annuals for nematodes (knots on the roots). Check houseplants for spider mites, scale and mealy bugs.

PRUNE: After blooming, chysanthemums should be cut back almost to the ground. Prune long, gangly shoots on shrubs. Remove dead and damaged wood from shrubs and trees.

LENGTHEN THE GROWING SEASON

To get the most out of a garden, you can extend the growing season by sheltering plants from cold weather both in early spring and during the fall. There are many ways to lengthen the growing season, and your choice depends on the amount of time and money you want to invest.

Cold frames and hot beds: Cold frames, sun boxes, and hot beds are relatively inexpensive, simple structures providing a favorable environment for growing cool-weather crops in the very early spring, the fall, and even into the winter months.

Cloches, Tunnels, and Row Covers: The cloche (pronounced klosh) was originally a bell-shaped glass jar set over delicate plants to protect them from the elements. The definition has expanded, however, to include many types of portable structures that shelter plants from drying winds and cold air.

Floating Row Covers: Row covers are a more recent development in extending vegetable production past frost dates. They are simple devices, pieces of material (in spunbonded polyesters) laid over transplants in the field. As the plants grow taller, the plants push up the material. Row covers retain heat and protect against frost so crops can be planted earlier in the spring and harvested later in the fall. They have demonstrated insect and vertebrate pest protection while also protecting plants from wind damage. Row covers generally provide four to five degrees of frost protection, so cool-season crops can be planted in air temperatures as low as 28° F.

Hotcaps: Hotcaps function as miniature greenhouses, trapping the heat from solar radiation. An effective hotcap transmits sufficient solar energy for photosynthesis and for warming the air inside, but not so much that overheating damages the plant. Hotcaps also must retain sufficient heat throughout the night to protect plants against low-temperature injury. Hotcap designs vary from wax paper cones to water-filled, plastic tepees.

Shading: It is not always easy to start seeds or young plants for fall crops in the hot and dry conditions of August. One simple way to provide shade in otherwise exposed conditions is to build a portable shade frame for placing over rows after seeds are sown or transplants are set out. This can be the same type of frame used for starting early seeds, but using lath strips or an old bamboo shade instead of plastic.

Greenhouses: The ultimate for year-round growing. Plan carefully before you buy and select one suited to your particular gardening needs.

Under Lights: Four-tube fluorescent fixtures are ideal for starting seeds. Regular tubes work just fine at a fraction of the cost of 'grow lights.' Overwinter tender plants with these lights, too.

PROTECTING PLANTS FROM FROSTS AND FREEZES

Frosts and freezes can wipe out a garden planting, especially when they come too early in the fall or late in the spring. Luckily, many of our garden vegetables such as cabbage, broccoli, Brussels sprouts, carrots, English peas, mustard, turnips and collards can tolerate a hard frost without much protection. Others, like our warm season vegetables, will be destroyed with even a moderate frost. When the temperatures fall to the critical point or just below, steps may be taken to prevent an otherwise total disaster. Here are some measures you can take to help hedge against frost:

Remove mulches that can act as a barrier against soil heat absorption as well as heat release. During the day, the sun will heat up the soil, providing plants with a source of heat overnight.

Water enough to adequately moisten the soil in the afternoon prior to a freeze. Avoid drowning the plants. Adding 10% moisture to the top 6" of soil increases heat-holding capacity by 50%.

Cover plants with blankets to trap the heat rising up from the ground. This practice alone can protect tender plants down to 28 degrees or less. Make sure to place weights around the edges to hold them down against the soil. Do not use plastic. If plastic touches the plant, that part will freeze.

Place a source of heat under blankets or other covers. Blankets do not make anything warm, they simply trap heat. Adding a heat source such as a string of Christmas lights or a suspended light bulb may help. Caution: do not let a hot bulb come into contact with any tender plant tissues or get wet. Fire and electrical shorts can occur! Check wires for bare spots and faulty light fixtures.

AVERAGE FIRST FALL FROST DATE IS NOVEMBER 28.

Protect tender vegetables and plants through the use of season extenders (this page), or harvest and process all ripe produce before the first frost.

There are many ways to bring wild birds into your garden:

- Provide plenty of food by planting herbaceous plants, shrubs and trees. Add hanging feeders.
- Provide water (preferably running) for drinking and bathing (use a shallow dish).
- Provide an area with a brush pile for cover and nesting.

BIRD-ATTRACTING PLANTS

Blackberry, Buckthorn, American Beautyberry, Cedar, Cherry Laurel, Dogwood, Drummond Red Maple, Fringe Tree, Grasses, American and Chinese Holly, Mulberry, Muscadine Grape, Possumhaw Holly, Oaks, Pecan, Persimmon, Pyracantha, Sunflower, Rusty Blackhaw Viburnum, Virginia Creeper, Yaupon Holly (red berries on female tree)

For more information:
Travis Audubon Society
www.travisaudubon.org/

Texas Parks and Wildlife Department
Texas Wildscapes Program
(800) 792-1112 (512) 389-4800
www.tpwd.state.tx.us/huntwild/wild/wildscapes

BIRDS' FAVORITE FOODS

Sunflower Seed (birds seem to prefer black-oil sunflower seed):

Blue Jay	Indigo Bunting
Chickadee	Nuthatch
Cardinal	Pine Siskin
Goldfinch	Tufted Titmouse
Grosbeak	Woodpecker

Suet (use suet cakes designed to withstand summer heat):

Blue Jay	Nuthatch
Brown Creeper	Tufted Titmouse
Cardinal	Woodpecker
Chickadee	Wren
Flicker	

Peanut Butter and Nutmeats:

Blue Jay	Nuthatch
Cardinal	Pine Warbler
Chickadee	Sparrow
Doves	Starling
Grackle	Tufted Titmouse
Grosbeak	Woodpecker
Finch	

Fruit (berries, chopped apples, banana, raisins, oranges):

Bluebird	Oriole
Blue Jay	Robin
Cardinal	Starling
Cedar Waxwing	Thrush
Hermit Thrush	Thrasher
Mockingbird	Woodpecker

Other Foods:

Millet:	**Corn:**
Blackbird	Bobwhite
Cowbird	Dove
Dove	Grackle
Sparrow	Jay
Towhee	Sparrow
	Starling

DIMENSIONS FOR BIRD HOUSES

SPECIES	LENGTH AND WIDTH INCHES	DEPTH OF CAVITY INCHES	FROM ENTRANCE TO FLOOR INCHES	DIAMETER OF ENTRANCE INCHES	HEIGHT ABOVE GROUND FEET
BLUEBIRD	5 X 5	8	6	1 1/5	5 TO 10
CHICKADEE	4 X 4	8 TO 10	6 TO 8	1 1/8	6 TO 15
TITMOUSE	4 X 4	8 TO 10	6 TO 8	1 1/4	6 TO 15
NUTHATCH	4 X 4	8 TO 10	6 TO 8	1 1/4	12 TO 20
HOUSE WREN	4 X 4	6 TO 8	1 TO 6	1 1/4	6 TO 10
CAROLINA WREN	4 X 4	6 TO 8	1 TO 6	1 1/5	6 TO 10
PURPLE MARTIN	6 X 6	6 TO 8	1	2 1/5	15 TO 20
FLICKER	7 X 7	16 TO 18	14 TO 16	2 1/5	6 TO 20
GOLDEN-FRONTED WOODPECKER	6 X 6	12 TO 15	9 TO 12	2	12 TO 20

DECEMBER

1	
2	
3	
4	
5	
6	
7	
8	
9	
10	
11	
12	
13	
14	
15	
16	
17	
18	
19	
20	
21	
22	
23	
24	
25	
26	
27	
28	
29	
30	
31	

/garden notes

CHRISTMAS TREE CARE

Pick the freshest possible tree, with a minimum amount of needle drop. Cut 1 to 2 inches off the bottom of the trunk and soak in a bucket of cool water until ready to put in tree stand. Check water level daily.

Or use a living Christmas tree that can be planted in the landscape. Afghan pine is great for this use.

Inspect all electrical equipment such as lights before placing on the Christmas tree and outside. Have a safe and Merry Holiday Season.

BEST HOUSE PLANTS TO CLEAN THE AIR

Areca Palm
Bamboo Palm
Boston Fern
Dracaena deremensis "*Warneckei*"
Dracaena "Janet Craig"
Dracaena fragrans "*Massangeana*"
Dracaena marginata
Dwarf Date Palm
English Ivy
Ficus Alii
Ficus benjamina
Florist's Mum
Gerbera Daisy
Golden Pothos
Kimberly Queen Fern
Lady Palm
Parlor Palm
Peace Lily
Red Emerald Philodendron
Rubber Plant
Schefflera
Syngoniym Diffenbackia "*Exotica Compacta*"

Source: *How to Grow Fresh Air: 50 Houseplants That Purify Your Home or Office* B. C. Wolverton

Holidays/Observations this month:
Christmas Day, Hanukkah, Kwanzaa, Boxing Day, New Year's Eve

THINGS TO PLANT IN DECEMBER

FLOWER PLANTS: Alyssum, Butterfly Weed, Calendula, Candytuft, Cornflower, Dianthus, Daisy (African, Michaelmas and Painted), Liatris, Nasturtium, Ornamental Cabbage and Kale, Phlox paniculata, Snapdragon, Stock.

FLOWER SEEDS: Bluebonnet, Calendula, Candytuft, Cornflower, Feverfew, Gaillardia, Gayfeather, Larkspur, Nasturtium, Poppy, Sweet Pea.

BULBS: Agapanthus, Allium, Alstroemeria, Amarcrinum, Amaryllis (in container), Crinum, Hyacinth, Liriope, Monkey Grass, Muscari, Star of Bethlehem (Orthinogalum), Rain Lily, Society Garlic, Spraxis, Aztec Lily (Sprekelia), Watsonia.

VEGETABLES:
ALL Month: Lettuce, Radish, Spinach
Protect cool-season vegetables from hard freezes with row covers.

FRUIT: Bare root or container-grown pecans, fruit trees, grapes and berry bushes.

THINGS TO DO IN DECEMBER

FERTILIZE: Fertilize bulbs with bone meal in the planting hole. Feed winter bloomers such as alyssum, dianthus and especially pansies every 4-6 weeks.

WATER: Water everything well before a freeze to protect against cold injury, but avoid overwatering.

TRANSPLANT: Transplant bare root and container grown roses, shrubs, trees, groundcovers and vines so they get established before warm weather arrives next summer.

PREPARE SOIL: Prepare dormant beds for spring planting: clean out dead and spent plants, compost to enrich the organic content of the soil. Send in soil samples (forms available at the Travis County Agrilife Extension Office). Check winter mulch and replenish, if needed. Stockpile leaves for mulching and composting throughout spring and summer.

LAWN CARE: Run mower and trimmer engines dry of gasoline, drain and change oil. Take them to the repair shop now to avoid the spring rush. Clean and oil ALL tools before storing for winter.

DISEASES/PESTS TO LOOK FOR: Watch for scale, mealy bugs and spider mites on houseplants. Root rot fungus thrives on over-watered houseplants.

OTHER THINGS TO DO

Time to get the garden ready for the new growing season. Clean, repair and replace garden tools. Create a garden plan to help organize your chores and planting schedules. Recycle your Christmas tree. Contact the Travis County Agrilife Extension Office (512-854-9600) for more information on Christmas tree recycling. As an alternative to the traditional Christmas tree, try a container tree or shrub (conically shaped) to be planted in your landscape later. Order spring vegetable seeds now. Remember the gardeners you know with gifts of tools, apparel, yard art or books (perhaps a copy of this **Garden Guide for Austin & Vicinity**. Contact The **Travis County Master Gardeners Association** at www.tcmastergardeners.org to order additional copies.)

**Need help with a Gardening Question? Call our Master Gardeners Help Desk:
512-854-9600 Monday-Friday, 9 am-5 pm
or visit our website: www.tcmastergardeners.org or email: travismg@ag.tamu.edu**

POISONOUS PLANTS

Vegetation helps sustain life. We eat many plants and herbs in our daily diet. But, we must remember to be choosy. Some plants, trees or shrubs are potential killers. Some part of the ornamental plants or flowers in your yard may contain deadly poison. Many poisonous plants are so common and seemingly innocuous, you do not suspect their toxic qualities.

For example, who would suspect that the beautiful oleander bush, grown outdoors all over the country, contains a deadly heart stimulant, similar to the drug digitalis? So powerful is this poison that a single leaf of an oleander can kill a child. And, people have died merely from eating steaks speared on oleander twigs and roasted over a fire.

It is easy to be deceived by plants. . .one part may be edible while another is poisonous. The following lists some of the more common poisonous plants, many of which can be found in Central Texas:

PLANT/TOXIC PART/SYMPTOMS

HOUSE PLANTS

Dieffenbachia (Dumb Cane), Elephant Ear/ All parts/intense burning and irritation of the mouth and tongue. Death can occur if base of the tongue swells enough to block the air passage of the throat.

Hyacinth, Narcissus, Daffodil/Bulbs/Nausea, vomiting, diarrhea. May be fatal.

Rosary Pea, Castor Bean/Seeds/**Fatal**. A single Rosary Pea seed has caused death. One or two Castor Bean seeds are near the lethal dose for adults.

FLOWER GARDEN PLANTS

Autumn Crocus, Star of Bethlehem/Bulbs/ vomiting and nervous excitement.

Bleeding Heart/foliage, roots/may be poisonous in large amounts. Has proved fatal to cattle.

Foxglove/leaves/large amounts cause dangerously irregular heartbeat and pulse, usually digestive upset and mental confusion. May be fatal.

Iris/Underground stems/severe, but not usually serious, digestive upset.

Larkspur/young plant, seeds/digestive upset, nervous excitement, depression. May be fatal.

Lily-of-the-Valley/leaves, flowers/irregular heart beat and pulse, usually accompanied by digestive upset and mental confusion.

Monkshood/fleshy roots/digestive upset and nervous excitement.

VEGETABLE GARDEN PLANTS

Rhubarb/Leaf blade/**Fatal**. Large amounts of raw or cooked leaves can cause convulsions, coma, followed rapidly by death. Stems only are edible.

ORNAMENTAL PLANTS

Daphne/Berries/**Fatal**. A few berries can kill a child.

Golden Chain/Bean-like capsules in which the seeds are suspended/severe poisoning. Excitement, staggering, convulsions and coma. May be fatal.

Laurels, Rhododendrons, Azaleas/All parts/ **Fatal**. Produces nausea and vomiting, depression, difficult breathing, prostration and coma.

Jasmine/Berries/**Fatal**. Digestive disturbance and nervous symptoms.

Lantana camara/Green berries/**Fatal**. Affects lungs, kidneys, heart and nervous system. Grows in the southern U.S..

Oleander/Leaves, branches/***EXTREMELY POISONOUS***. Affects the heart, produces severe digestive upset and has caused death.

Wisteria/Seeds, pods/mild to severe digestive upset. Children can be poisoned by this plant.

Yew/Berries, foliage/**Fatal**. Foliage more toxic than berries. Death is usually sudden without warning symptoms.

Sago Palm/All parts/**Fatal**. Causes vomiting, diarrhea, loss of appetite, and liver failure.

TREES AND SHRUBS

Black Locust/Bark, sprouts, foliage/children have suffered nausea, weakness and depression after chewing the bark and seeds.

Elderberry/All parts, especially roots/children have been poisoned by using pieces of the pithy stems for blowguns. Nausea and digestive upset.

Oaks/Foliage, acorns/affects kidneys gradually. Symptoms appear only after several days or weeks. Takes a large amount for poisoning.

Wild and cultivated cherries/Twigs, foliage/ **Fatal**. Contains a compound that releases cyanide when eaten. Gasping, excitement and prostration are common symptoms.

PLANTS IN WOODED AREAS

Jack-in-the-Pulpit/All parts, especially roots/ contain small needle-like crystals of calcium oxalate that cause intense irritation and burning of the mouth and tongue.

Moonseed/Berries blue, purple color, resembling wild grapes. ***May be fatal.***

Mayapple/Apple, foliage, roots/contains at least 16 active toxic principles, primarily in the roots. Children often eat the apple with no ill effects, but several apples may cause diarrhea.
Mistletoe/Berries/**Fatal**. Both children and adults have died from eating the berries.

PLANTS IN SWAMP/MOIST AREAS

Water Hemlock/All parts/**Fatal**. Violent and painful convulsions. A number of people have died from hemlock.

PLANTS IN FIELDS

Buttercups/All parts/irritant juices may severely injure the digestive system.
Jimson Weed (Thorn Apple)/All parts/abnormal thirst, distorted sight, delirium, incoherence and coma. Common cause of poisoning. Has proved fatal.
Nightshade/All parts, especially the unripened berry/**Fatal**. Intense digestive disturbance and nervous symptoms.
Poison Hemlock/All parts/**Fatal**. Resembles a large wild carrot.

Treat unknown plants with respect, and teach your children to do the same.

Phone Number for Poison Center
1-800-222-1222

Reprinted from materials provided by the Texas State Department of Health and the National Safety Council.

A Field Guide to Venomous Animals and Poisonous Plants: North America North of Mexico by Roger Caras, Steven Foster

Cornell University Poisonous Plants Informational Database: http://www.ansci.cornell.edu/plants/

Common Poisonous Houseplants: www. http://www.nybg.org/plants/factsheets/poison.html

ALLERGY-CAUSING PLANTS

Pollens from some plants (usually airborne) can cause allergic reactions. Insect-pollinated plants with large, sticky pollen seldom cause these problems.

The following trees, shrubs, plants and grasses are insect-pollinated and cause fewer problems for most people with allergies:

Apple	Dusty Miller	Petunia
Alyssum	Geranium	Phlox
Azalea	Hibiscus	Plum
Begonia	Hosta	Rose
Boxwood	Hyacinth	Salvia
Cacti	Hydrangea	Snapdragon
Cherry	Impatiens	St. Augus-
Clematis	Iris	tine Grass
Columbine	Lilac	Sunflower
Crocus	Lily	Tulip
Daffodil	Magnolia	Verbena
Daisy	Narcissus	Vibirnum
Dahlia	Pansy	Zinnia
Dogwood	Pear	

These trees, plants and grasses are wind-pollinated and more likely to cause allergy problems:

Alder	Fescue	Pine
Ash	Hickory	Popular
Aspen	Johnson grass	Redtop
Beech	Juniper	Saltgrass
Bermuda	Maple	Sweet Olive
grass	Mulberry	Sycamore
Birch	Oak	Timothy
Box Elder	Olive	Walnut
Cedar	Orchard	Willow
Cottonwood	Palm	
Cypress	Pecan	
Elm	Perennial rye	

Weeds, like ragweed, pigweed and Russian thistle, are common in the United States and are highly allergenic. In most cases, weeds are unavoidable. Allergists also recommend wearing a mask when gardening, leaving all gardening tools (including clothing) outdoors and showering immediately after working outdoors to help control allergic reactions.

Taking these steps and avoiding the appropriate plants can make it possible for the allergy sufferer to enjoy being outdoors in the spring.

For additional information:
Allergy Free Gardening by Thomas Ogren
www.allergyfree-gardening.com

Aggie Horticulture
http://aggie-horticulture.tamu.edu
http://aggie-horticulture.tamu.edu/travis

Austin Area Garden Centers
http://aggie-horticulture.tamu.edu/travis/r_garden.htm

Austin Energy Green Builder Program
512-482-5300 http://austinenergy.com/wps/portal/aegb/home

Austin Habitat for Humanity
310 Comal Street Suite 100, Austin, TX 78702
512-472-8788 www.austinhabitat.org

Austin Sierra Club
austinsierraclub@gmail.com
https://texas2.sierraclub.org/austin/

Bat Conservation International
512-327-9721 www.batcon.org

Certified Farmers Markets
Statewide Listing of Farmers Markets and Pick Your Own Growers http://www.gotexan.org/LocateGOTEXAN/CertifiedFarmersMarkets.aspx

Community Supported Agriculture
Find a farmers market near you
http://www.localharvest.org/csa/

Conservation Priorities For Texas
www.texasep.org/cpft

Firewise Communities
www.firewise.org

Go Texan Marketing Texas Products
www.gotexan.org

Green Corn Project
Box 49468, Austin, TX 78765
www.greencornproject.org

Grow Green
www.growgreen.org
Native & Adapted Plant list for Austin area and gardening education

Hornsby Bend-Bird Observatory
www.hornsbybend.org

hortIPM Information on Integrated Pest Management http://hortipm.tamu.edu

Integrated Pest Management
http://austintexas.gov/ipm

Jordan-Bachman Pioneer Farm
10621 Pioneer Farm Drive
Austin, Tx 78754
512-837-1215
www.pioneerfarms.org

Keep Austin Beautiful
www.keepaustinbeautiful.org

Lady Bird Johnson Wildflower Center
4801 LaCrosse Ave., Austin, TX 78739
512-232-0100 www.wildflower.org

Master Gardeners Program/Texas AgriLife Extension-Travis County
1600-/B Smith Road
Austin, TX 78721 512-854-9600
www.tcmastergardeners.org

McKinney Roughs Nature Park
512-303-5073 or 800-776-LCRA, Ext. 8021
www.lcra.org/parks/developed_parks/mckinney_roughs.html

National Sustainable Agriculture, Community Supported Agriculture
www.attra.org/attra-pub/csa.html

National Wildlife Federation Backyard Habitat nwf.org/backyard

National Wildlife Federation (field guides and park & refuge information) www.eNature.com

Native Plant Society of Texas
320 W. San Antonio Street
P.O. Box 3017
Fredericksburg, TX 78624-1929
830-997-9272 www.npsot.org/wp

Native Prairies Association of Texas
415 N. Guadalupe Street, PMB 385
San Marcos, TX 78666
512-772-4741 www.texasprairie.org

Nature Conservancy of Texas
P.O. Box 1440, San Antonio, TX 78295-1440
(210) 224-8774 nature.org/wherewework/northamerica/states/texas/preserves/art25166.html

Organic Certification-Texas Department of Agriculture http://www.texasagriculture.gov/regulatoryprograms/organics.aspx

Plant Conservation Alliance
Bureau of Land Management 1849 C Street NW, Rm 2134LM, Attention: Olivia Kwong, Washington, DC 20240 202-912-7232
http://www.nps.gov/plants

South Austin Community Gardens
2800 S. 5th St.
http://www.main.org/sacgarden

State Farmers Market Representative
Jim Jones, Texas Dept. of Agriculture
Box 12847, Austin, TX 78711
jjones@agr.state.tx.us

Sunshine Community Gardens
4814 Sunshine Drive, Austin, TX 78756
512-458-2009
http://www.sunshinecommunitygardens.org

Sustainable Food Center
2921 E. 17th Street, Building C, Austin, TX 78702
512-236-0074
http://www.sustainablefoodcenter.org

Texas Agrilife Extension-Travis County
1600-B Smith Road
Austin, TX 78721 512-854-9600
http://travis-tx.tamu.edu

Texas Commission on Environmental Quality (TCEQ)
512-239-1000 http://www.tceq.state.tx.us

Texas Department of Agriculture
1700 North Congress Avenue
Stephen F. Austin Building, 11th Floor
Austin, TX 78701 512-463-7476
http://www.texasagriculture.gov

Texas Evapotranspiration from TexasET
http://texaset.tamu.edu contains weather information, evapotranspiration, and crop watering recommendations of the Agriculture Program: http://agrilife.org/ of the Texas A&M University System

Texas Master Naturalist Program
http://txmn.org/

Texas Nursery & Landscape Association
7730 S. IH 35, Austin, TX 78745
512-280-5182 http://txnla.org

CALL BEFORE YOU DIG
Provides a convenient method of finding out where all your underground utilities are located before you dig. Call the state-wide Notification Center at 1-800-545-6005. Operators are on duty 24-hours a day, seven days a week (excluding legal holidays).

Texas Oak Wilt Information Partnership
http://www.texasoakwilt.org

Texas Organic Farmers & Gardeners Association http://www.tofga.org

Texas Parks and Wildlife Department
4200 Smith School Road, Austin, TX 78744
General Information Line 1-800-792-1112
http://www.tpwd.state.tx.us

Texas Water Development Board Rainwater Harvesting http://www.twdb.texas.gov/innovativewater/rainwater

Texas Wildscapes
(Austin area) 512-389-4800
http://www.tpwd.state.tx.us/huntwild/wild/wildscapes

Texas Wine Marketing http://www.gotexanwine.org

Travis Audubon Society
3710 Cedar Street, Box 5
Austin, Tx 78705
512-300-2473 http://www.travisaudubon.org

Tree Folks
Box 704, Austin, TX 78767
512-443-5323 http://www.treefolks.org

Water Conservation Program
Box 1088, Austin, TX 78767 512-974-2199
http://www.austintexas.gov/department/water-conservation (watering schedule & rebates)

Watershed Protection & Development Review Department
512-974-2550
http://www.austintexas.gov/department/watershed-protection

WaterWise Council of Texas
http://www.waterwisetexas.org

Wild Basin Wilderness Preserve
805 N. Capital of Texas Hwy, Austin, TX 78746
512-327-7622 http://www.wildbasin.org

For information on Farmer's Markets:
http://austin.1thingus.com/the-real-taste-of-greater-austin/

Other helplful links on Farmer's Markets:
http://www.localharvest.org/austin-tx/farmers-markets/
http://www.gotexan.org/LocateGOTEXAN/CertifiedFarmersMarkets/Austin.aspx
http://www.edibleaustin.com/index.php/farmers-markets

For information on Farms and Farm Stands:
http://www.pickyourown.org/TXaustin.htm

Other helpful link on Farms and Farm Stands:
http://www.localharvest.org/organic-farms/

For information on CSAs:
http://www.localharvest.org/austin-tx/csa/

FARM STANDS

Arnosky Family Farm (Texas Specialty Cut Flowers) Corner of RR165 and RR2325 (8 mi. from Blanco). Open Saturdays 9 am-5pm (flowers and vegetables). 830-833-5428 www.texascolor.com

Bastrop Garden Farms
316 Old Highway 71 (Country Rd. 335). Cedar Creek, TX 78612. 512-303-5672 www.bastropgardens.com

Bella Vista Ranch
3101 Mount Sharp Road, Wimberley, TX 78676. Open Saturdays 10 am-5pm 512-847-6514 www.bvranch.com

Boggy Creek Farm (Certified Organic)
3414 Lyons Road, Austin, TX 78702
512-926-4650 www.boggycreekfarm.com
boggycrk@realtime.com

Green Gate Farm (Farm Stand and U-Pick)
8604 FM 969 (Decker Lane at MLK), Austin, TX. Open March-December noon-dark (call first). 512-929-2436

Pure Luck Organic Farm & AA Dairy (Certified Organic). Will open to public again in Fall 2009 101 Twin Oaks Trail, Dripping Springs, TX 78620 512-858-7034 www.purelucktexas.com

Sweet Berry Farm
1.5 miles north of FM 1431 on FM 1980 Marble Falls, TX 78654 830-798-1462 www.sweetberryfarm.com

FARMS THAT OFFER SUBSCRIPTION SHARES

Finca Pura Vida LLC
944 Lakeview Road, Fayetteville, TX 78940
979-249-3866 www.fincapurvida.org

Hairston Creek Farm (Certified Organic)
4300 County Rd. 335, Burnet, TX 78611
512-756-8380 www.hairstoncreekfarm.com

Home Sweet Farm
7800 FM 2502, Brenham, TX 77833
979-251-9922 www.homesweetfarm.com

Johnson's Backyard Garden
9515 Hergotz Lane, Box E, Austin, TX 78742
512-389-2515 www.johnsonsbackyardgarden.com

McKemie HomeGrown
Rt 2, Box 348, Dale, TX 78616 512-764-2122
www.austinfarm.org/homegrown

Milberg Farm (Certified Organic)
737 Opal Ln., Kyle, TX 78640
512-268-1433 www.localharvest.org

Steele Farms (Seguin, TX)
www.freshtexasproduce.com

Tecolote Farm
16301 Decker Lake Road, Manor, TX 78653
512-276-7008 www.localharvest.com
telecotefarm@juno.com (e-mail preferred)

Walnut Creek Farm
126 Walnut Creek Cove, Bastrop, TX 78602 512-303-3400 www.wcorganic.com
johnpaquin01@aol.com

WHAT'S IN SEASON MONTH BY MONTH

January
Broccoli, Carrots, Greenhouse Vegetables, Greens, Herbs, Mushrooms, Turnips

February
Carrots, Greenhouse Vegetables, Greens, Herbs, Mushrooms, Turnips

March
Carrots, Greenhouse Vegetables, Greens, Herbs, Mushrooms, Turnips,

April
Cabbage, Carrots, Green Onions, Greenhouse Vegetables, Greens, Herbs, Mushrooms, Spinach, Turnips

May
Blueberries, Cabbage, Green Onions, Greenhouse Vegetables, Greens, Herbs, Mushrooms, Onions, Peas-Field, Peppers-Bell, Peppers-Chili, Potatoes, Spinach, Squash, Tomatoes, Turnips

June
Blueberries, Cabbage, Cantaloupes, Cucumbers, Greens, Onions, Herbs, Mushrooms, Onions, Peas-Field, Peaches, Peppers-Bell, Peppers-Chili, Potatoes, Squash, Tomatoes, Watermelons

July
Apples, Cabbage, Cantaloupes, Cucumbers, Herbs, Honeydew Melons, Mushrooms, Onions, Peas-Field, Peaches, Peppers-Chili, Potatoes, Squash, Watermelons

August
Apples, Cabbage, Cantaloupes, Cucumbers, Herbs, Honeydew Melons, Mushrooms, Onions, Peas-Field, Peaches, Potatoes, Squash, Sweet Potatoes, Watermelons

September
Apples, Cabbage, Cantaloupes, Cucumbers, Herbs, Honeydew, Melons, Mushrooms, Peas-Field, Potatoes, Pumpkins, Squash, Sweet Potatoes, Turnips, Watermelons

October
Apples, Cabbage, Cantaloupes, Cucumbers, Greenhouse Vegetables, Greens, Herbs, Honeydew Melons, Mushrooms, Peas-Field, Peppers-Bell, Potatoes, Squash, Sweet Potatoes, Turnips, Watermelons

November
Broccoli, Carrots, Cucumbers, Greenhouse Vegetables, Greens, Herbs, Honeydew Melons, Mushrooms, Peas-Field, Peppers-Bell, Squash, Sweet Potatoes, Turnips

December
Broccoli, Carrots, Greenhouse Vegetables, Greens, Herbs, Mushrooms, Peppers-Bell, Sweet Potatoes, Turnips

ZILKER BOTANICAL GARDEN

2220 Barton Springs Road, Austin, TX 78746 www.zilkergarden.org
Below is a list of the Garden Clubs affiliated with the Austin Area Garden Council, Inc.
Meetings are held at Zilker Botanical Garden unless otherwise noted.
Call The Austin Area Garden Center for more information: 512-477-8672.

Austin Area Begonia Society
4th Sunday @ 2 pm (except December)

Austin Area Creative Designers
3rd Thursday @ 1 pm

Austin Bonsai Society
www.austinbonsaisociety.com
2nd Wednesday @ 7 pm
Study group meets 3rd Tuesday @ 7:30 pm

Austin Butterfly Forum
www.austinbutterflies.org
4th Monday @ 7 pm (except Jul, Aug & Dec)

Austin Cactus & Succulent Society
www.austincss.com
3rd Thursday @ 7:30 pm

Austin Daylily Society
1st Thursday @ 7 pm (except Dec, Jan, Jun, & Jul)

Austin Herb Society
www.austinherbsociety.org
1st Tuesday @ 9:30 am (except August)

Austin Ikebana Study Group
1st Friday @ 9:30 am

Austin Organic Gardeners
www.main.org/aog
2nd Monday @ 6:30 pm

Austin Pond Society
www.austinpondsociety.org/
3rd Monday @ 7 pm (except December)

Austin Rose Society
3rd Tuesday @ 7 pm

Barton Hills Garden Club
4th Tuesday September - May @ 9:30 am

Capitol City Judges Council
2nd Wednesday @ 9:30 am (September-May)

Docents of Zilker Botanical Gardens
4th Saturday @ 9:30 am

East Austin Garden Club
4th Saturday @ 9:30 am
Call 512-477-8672 for location.

First Austin African Violet Society
www.faavs.org
4th Wednesday @ 9:30 am

The Garden Club of Austin
www.thegardenclubofaustin.org
4th Thursday @ 7 pm

Heart O'Texas Orchid Society
www.hotos.org
1st Tuesday @ 7 pm

Heart of the Hills Garden Club
3rd Tuesday @ 9:30 am (Sept-May)

Iris Society of Austin
2nd Tuesday @ 7:30 pm (Sept-May, except Dec)

The Optimistic Garden Club
3rd Thursday, 9:45 am (Sept-May)

Porcelain Art Club of Texas
1st Monday @ 9:30 am (October-May); 2nd Monday @ 9:30 am (January and September)

Texas Bamboo Society
http://texasbamboosociety.com
3rd Saturday, 9:30-noon
Please call for location: 512-906-8250

Town Lake Garden Club
2nd Thursday @ 10 am (September - May, except January)

Travis County Beekeepers Association
www.facebook.com/TravisCountyBeeks

Travis County Master Gardeners Association
512-854-9600 www.tcmastergardeners.org
1st Wednesday @ 7 pm

Violet Crown Garden Club
www.violetcrowngardenclub.org
4th Thursday @ 9:30 am

West Lake Hills Garden Club
3rd Tuesday (offsite)

Western Trails Garden Club
2nd Friday @ 11 am (offiste, September - May)

Yaupon Garden Club
3rd Wednesday @ 10 am (September - May)

Zilker Garden Club
4th Tuesday @ 9:30 am (September - May)

TEXAS BOTANICAL GARDENS

Bayou Bend Collection and Gardens
6300 Memorial Dr. @ Westcott St., Houston, TX 77007
713-639-7750 www.mfah.org/bayoubend

Botanical Research Institute of Texas
1700 University Drive, Fort Worth, TX 76107
817-332-4441 www.brit.org

Carleen Bright Arboretum
1 Pavilion Way, Woodway, TX 76712
254-399-9204
www.woodway-texas.com/carleen-bright-arboretum/

Dallas Arboretum & Botanical Society, Inc.
8525 Garland Rd., Dallas, TX 75218
214-515-6615 www.dallasarboretum.org

Fort Worth Botanic Garden
3220 Botanic Garden Blvd., Fort Worth, TX 76107
817-392-5510 www.fwbg.org

Heard Natural Science Museum & Wildlife Sanctuary, 1 Nature Place, McKinney, TX 75069
972-562-5566 www.heardmuseum.org

Houston Arboretum & Nature Center
4501 Woodway Dr., Houston, TX 77024
713-681-8433 http://houstonarboretum.org

Stephen F. Austin Mast Arboretum
Stephen F. Austin State University
13000 - SFA Station (Wilson Drive)
Nacogdoches, TX 75962
936-468-1832 arboretum.sfasu.edu

Mercer Arboretum & Botanic Gardens
22306 Aldine-Westfield Road, Humble, TX 77338
281-443-8731 www.hcp4.net/mercer/index.htm

Moody Gardens
One Hope Blvd., Galveston, TX 77554
800-582-4673 www.moodygardens.com

San Antonio Botanical Gardens
555 Funston Place, San Antonio, TX 78209
210-207-3250 www.sabot.org

South Texas Botanical Gardens & Nature Ctr.
8548 S. Staples St., Corpus Christi, TX 78413
361-852-2100 www.stxbot.org

Texas Discovery Gardens
3601 Martin Luther King Blvd., Dallas, TX 75210
214-428-7476, x341 www.texasdiscoverygardens.org

Zilker Botanical Garden
2220 Barton Springs Rd., Austin, TX 78746
512-477-8672 www.zilkergarden.org

OTHER GARDENS TO SEE

Antique Rose Emporium
10,000 Hwy 50, Brenham, TX 77833
979-836-5548
www.antiqueroseemporium.com

Fredericksburg Herb Farm
405 Whitney, Fredericksburg, TX 78624
830-997-8615 www.fredericksburgherbfarm.com

Lady Bird Johnson Wildflower Center
4801 La Crosse Ave., Austin, TX 78739
512-232-0100 www.wildflower.org

McAshan Herb Gardens at Festival Hill, The
248 Jaster Road, Round Top, TX 78954
Herb Events: 979-249-3129
www.festivalhill.org

Natural Gardener, The
8648 Old Bee Caves Rd., Austin, TX 78735
512-288-6113 www.naturalgardeneraustin.com

Peckerwood Gardens
20559 FM 359, Hempstead, TX 77445
979-826-3232 www.peckerwoodgarden.com

Tyler Rose Festival/Tyler Rose Museum
420 Rose Park Dr., Tyler TX 75702 903-597-3130
www.texasrosefestival.com/

Wildseed Farms
100 Legacy Drive, Fredericksburg, TX 78624
800-848-0078 www.wildseedfarms.com

Backbone Valley Nursery
4201 FM 1980, Marble Falls, TX 78654
830-693-9348 www.backbonevalleynursery.com/

Barton Springs Nursery
3601 Bee Caves Rd., Austin, TX 78746
512-328-6655 www.bartonspringsnursery.net

Bastrop Gardens
316 Old 71 (CR 335), Cedar Creek, TX 78612
512-303-5672 www.bastropgardens.com

Bloomers Garden Center
507 North Hwy. 95, Elgin, TX 78621
512-281-2020 www.bloomerselgin.com

Breed & Co.
3663 Bee Caves Rd., Austin, TX 78746
512-328-3960
718 W. 29th, Austin, TX 78705
512-474-6679 www.breedandco.com

Callahan's General Store
501 South Highway 183, Austin, TX 78741
512-385-3452 www.callanhansgeneralstore.com

Countryside Nursery
13292 Pond Springs Rd, Austin, TX 78729
512-249-0100 www.countrysideaustin.com

D&B Tree Company, Inc.
15000 RR 620 N, Austin, TX 78717
512-248-5555 www.dandbtreecompany.com

Dirt & Roses
128 FM 1441, Bastrop, TX 78602
512-308-9955 www.dirtnroses.com

East Austin Succulents
801 Tillery St, Austin, TX 78702
512-947-6531
www.facebook.com/east.austinsucculents

Eco-Wise
110 W. Elizabeth St., Austin, TX 78704
512-326-4474 www.ecowise.com/

Leaf Landscape Supply
5700 Hwy 290 West, Austin, TX 78735
512-288-5900 www.pondsandgarden.com

Gaddy's Feed Hardware & Garden
403 FM 685, Pflugerville, TX 78660
512-251-4428 www.gaddys.com

Garden-Ville Bee Cave
4001 Ranch Rd 620 S, Bee Cave, TX 78738
512-219-5311 www.garden-ville.com

Garden-Ville Buda / Creedmoor
3606 FM 1327 , Creedmoor, TX 78610
512-329-4900 www.garden-ville.com

Garden-Ville Georgetown
250 W.L. Walden Rd, Georgetown, TX 78626
512-930-8282 www.garden-ville.com

Garden-Ville San Marcos
2212 Ranch Road 12, San Marcos, TX 78666
512-754-0060 www.garden-ville.com

Geo Growers
12002-B Hwy. 290 West, Austin, TX 78737
512-288-4405 & 512-892-2722 www.geogrowers.net

Great Outdoors
2730 S. Congress Ave., Austin, TX 78704
512-448-2992 www.gonursery.com

Green 'N Growing
601 W. Pecan St., Pflugerville, TX 78660
512-251-3262 www.greenngrowing.com

Hill Country Water Gardens & Nursery
1407 North Bell Blvd. (Hwy 183 North)
Cedar Park, TX 78613 512-260-5050
www.hillcountrywatergardens.com/

It's About Thyme
11726 Manchaca Rd., Austin, TX 78748 until Fall 2016
(new) 2324 Bliss Spillar Rd., Manchaca, TX 78652
512-280-1192 www.itsaboutthyme.com

King Ranch Turfgrass-North Austin
7221 McNeil Drive, Austin, TX 78729
512-892-3636 www.krturfgrass.com

King Ranch Turfgrass-South Austin
5910 Hwy. 290 West, Austin, TX 78735
512-892-3636 www.krturfgrass.com

Living Desert Cactus Nursery
22701 Hwy 71 W. Spicewood, Texas 78669
866-927-8881

McIntire's Garden Center
303 Leander Rd., Georgetown, TX 78626
512-863-8243 www.mcintiresgarden.com/

The Natural Gardener
8648 Old Bee Caves Rd., Austin, TX 78735
512-288-6113 www.naturalgardeneraustin.com

Olde Thyme Gardens
950 CR 365, Taylor, TX 76574
512-352-3147
www.oldethymegardens.wordpress.com/

Red Barn Garden Center
12881 Pond Springs Rd., Austin, TX 78729
512-335-8093
www.redbarngardencenter.net

Round Rock Garden Center
901 Sam Bass Rd., Round Rock, TX 78681
512-255-3353 www.roundrockgardens.com

Shoal Creek Nursery
2710 Hancock Dr., Austin, TX 78731
512-458-5909 www.shoalcreeknursery.com

Sledd Nursery
1211 West Lynn St., Austin, TX 78703
512-478-9977 www.sleddnursery.com

Sol'stice Garden Expressions
900 West Hwy 290, Dripping Springs, TX 78620
512-858-7263 www.solsticegardens.com

Spicewood Spines
by appointment only
(830) 613-0703 www.spicewoodspines.com

Lakeway Garden Center, Inc.
21215 Hwy 71 West, Spicewood, TX 78669
512-263-5275 www.sunshineaustin.com

Ted's Trees
1118 Tillery St., Austin, TX 78702
512-928-8733 www.tedstrees.com

Tillery Street Plant Company
801 Tillery Street, Austin TX 78702
512-567-1090 www.tillerystreetplantcompany.com

AUSTIN-AREA NATURE ATTRACTIONS

Austin Nature & Science Center
2389 Stratford Dr., Zilker Park, Austin, TX 78746
512-974-3888 www.austintexas.gov/ansc

Austin Nature Preserves
Balcones Canyonland Preserve, Blunn Creek Preserve, Mayfield Park & Preserve, Karst Preserve, Spicewood Springs Preserve and Zilker Preserve. 512-974-9461.
www.austintexas.gov/department/nature-preserves-0

Jourdan/Bachman Pioneer Farm
10621 Pioneer Farms Drive, Austin, TX 78754
512-837-1215
www.pioneerfarms.org

Lady Bird Johnson Wildflower Center
4801 La Crosse Ave., Austin, TX 78739
512-232-0100 www.wildflower.org

McKinney Falls State Park
5808 McKinney Falls Pkwy., Austin, TX 78744
512-243-1643
tpwd.texas.gov/state-parks/mckinney-falls

McKinney Roughs
1884 Hwy 71 West, Cedar Creek, TX 78612
512-303-5073
www.lcra.org/parks/developed-parks/Pages/mckinney-roughs-nature-park.aspx

Umlauf Sculpture Garden & Museum
605 Robert E. Lee Rd., Austin, TX 78704
512-445-5582 www.umlaufsculpture.org/

Wild Basin Wilderness Preserve
805 North Capital of Texas Hwy, Austin, TX 78746
512-327-7622 www.wildbasin.org

Zilker Botanical Garden
2220 Barton Springs Rd., Austin, TX 78746
512-477-8672 www.zilkergarden.org

Zilker Park
2100 Barton Springs Rd., Austin, TX 78746
512-974-6700 www.austintexas.gov/department/zilker-metropolitan-park

FLOWERS

Antique Roses for the South (William C. Welch, 2004)

Bulbs for Warm Climates (Thad M. Howard, 2001)

Can't Miss Container Gardening (Felder Rushing, 2005)

Perennial Gardening in Texas (Alan Dean Franz, 2005)

Garden Bulbs for the South (Scott Ogden, 2007)

Passalong Plants (Steve Bender and Felder Rushing, 2002)

Perennial Garden Color (William C. Welch, 1989)

Perennial Gardens for Texas (Julie Ryan, 1998)

Plants for Texas (Howard Garrett, 1996)

The Bountiful Flower Garden: Growing and Sharing Cut Flowers in the South (William C. Welch, 2000)

The New Central Texas Gardener (Cheryl Hazeltine and Barry Lovelace, 1999)

The Texas Flowerscaper: A Seasonal Guide to Bloom, Height, Color, and Texture (Kathy Huber, 1996)

The Texas Flower Garden (Kathy Huber, 2005)

Tough-as-Nails Flowers for the South (Norman Winter, 2003)

GENERAL GARDENING

1001 Most Asked Texas Gardening Questions (Neil Sperry, 1997)

Animal, Vegetable, Miracle: A Year of Food Life (Barabara Kingsolver, Camille Kingsolver and Steven L. Hopp, 2007)

Complete Guide to Gardening (Susan A. Roth and Better Homes & Garden, 2001)

Complete Guide to Texas Gardening (Neil Sperry, 1991)

Gardening Southern Style (Felder Rushing, 1987)

Gardening Success with Difficult Soils: Limestone, Alkaline Clay and Caliche Soils (Scott Ogden, 1992)

Heirloom Gardening in the South (William C. Welch and Greg Grant, 2011)

Identification, Selection and Use of Southern Plants (Neil G. Odenwald and James R. Turner, 2006)

Month by Month Gardening in Texas (Robert "Skip" Richter, 2014)

Second Nature: A Gardener's Education (Michael Pollan, 2003)

Sunbelt Gardening: Success in Hot-Weather Climates (Tom Peace, 2000)

Teaming with Microbes: The Organic Gardener's Guide to the Soil Food Web (Jeff Lowenfels and Wayne Lewis, 2010)

Texas Garden Almanac (Month by Month Guide) (Doug Welsh, 2007)

Texas Gardening the Natural Way-The Complete Handbook (Howard Garrett, 2002)

Texas Organic Gardening (Howard Garrett, 2002)

Texas Public Gardens (Elvin McDonald, 2009)

The Lone Star Field Guide to Wildflowers, Trees and Shrubs (Delena Tull, 2003)

The Lone Star Gardener's Book of Lists (William D. Adams and Lois Trigg Chaplin, 2000)

The New Southern Living Garden Book (Steve Bender, 2015)

The Zone Garden 8-9-10 (Charlotte M Frieze, 1997)

Tough Plants for Southern Gardens (Felder Rushing, 2003)

Warm-Climate Gardening: Tips, Techniques, Plans, Projects for Humid or Dry Conditions (Barbara Pleasant, 1993)

HERBS

Herb Gardening in Texas (Sol Meltzer, 2006)

Herbs for Texas (Howard Garrett, 2001)

Southern Herb Growing (Madalene Hill, Jean Hardy and Gwen Barclay, 1997)

The Herb Garden Cookbook: The Complete Gardening and Gourmet Guide (Luncinda Hutson, 2003)

LANDSCAPING

Home Landscaping: Texas (Greg Grant and Roger Holmes, 2006)

Landscape Guide: The South-Central States Texas, Oklahome, Arkansas and Louisiana (Tom Clote, 2001)

Landscape Plants for Texas and Environs (Michael Aloysius Arnold, 2002)

Landscaping with Native Plants of Texas and the Southwest (George O. Miller, 2006)

Native Texas Plants: Landscaping Region by Region (Sally Wasowski, 2002)

Plant-Driven Design: Creating Gardens that Honor Plants, Place and Spirit (Scott Ogden and Lauren Springer Ogden, 2008)

The Intimate Garden (Brian D. Coleman, 2007)

The Perfect Texas Lawn: Attaining and Maintaining the Lawn You Want (Steve Dobbs, 2002)

PEST CONTROL

A Field Guide to Common Texas Insects (Bastiaan Drees and John Jackman, 1998)

Deerproofing Your Yard and Garden (Rhonda Massinghamm Hart, 2005)

Deer-Resistant Landscaping: Proven Advice and Strategies for Outwitting Deer and 20 Other Pesky Mammals (Neil Soderstrom, 2009)

Gardening in Deer Country: South and West: Zones 8-9-10 (Mia Amato, 2009)

Insects of Texas: A Practical Guide (David H. Kattes, 2009)

Southern Living Garden Problem Solver (Steve Bender, 1999)

Texas Bug Book: The Good, the Bad, and the Ugly (Malcolm Beck and J. Howard Garrett, 2005)

TREES

A Field Guide to Texas Trees (Benny J. Simpson, 2002)
Texas Trees (Howard Garrett, 2002)
Texas Trees: A Friendly Guide (Patty Leslie and Paul W. Cox, 1988)
Trees and Shrubs for Warm Climates: An Illustrated Encyclopedia (Michael Dirr, 2002)
Trees of Central Texas (Robert A. Vines, 1984)
Trees of Texas: An Easy Guide to Leaf Identification (Carmine A. Stahl and Ria McElvaney, 2003)
Trees, Shrubs and Vines of the Texas Hill Country: A Field Guide (Jan Wrede, 2005)
Trees, Shrubs & Woody Vines of East Texas (Elray S. Nixon, 2000)

VEGETABLES

All New Square Foot Gardening (Mel Batholomew, 2006)
Four Seasons Harvest: Organic Vegetables from Your Home Garden All Year Long (Eliot Coleman, Barbara Damrosch and Kathy Bray, 1999)
How to Grow More Vegetables (and Fruits, Nuts, Berries, Grains and Other Crops) Than You Ever Thought Possible on Less Land Than You Can Imagine (John Jeavons, 2006)
Texas Organic Vegetable Gardening: The Total Guide to Growing Vegetables, Fruits, Herbs and Other Edible Plants the Natural Way (J. Howard Garrett and C. Malcolm Beck, 1998)
Texas Tomato Lover's Handbook (William D. Adams, 2011)
The Southern Kitchen Garden: Vegetables, Fruits, Herbs and Flowers Essential for the Southern Cook (William D. Adams and Tom LeRoy, 2007)
The Vegetable Gardener's Bible (Edward C. Smith, 2000)
Vegetable Gardening in the Southwest (Trisha Shirey, 2015.)

WATER CONSERVATION

Requiem for a Lawnmower: Gardening in a Warmer, Drier World (Sally Wasowski, 2004)
The Water Saving Garden: How to Grow a Gorgeous Garden with a Lot Less Water (Pam Penick, 2016)
WaterWise Landscaping with Trees, Shrubs and Vines: A Xeriscape Guide for the Rocky Mountain Region, California and Desert Southwest (Jim Knopf, 2005)

WILDFLOWERS

Field Guide to the Broad-leaved Herbaceous Plants of South Texas: Used by Livestock and Wildlife (James H. Everitt, 1999)
Field Guide to the Wild Orchids of Texas (Paul Martin Brown and Stan Folsom, 2008)
Gardening with Native Plants of the South (Sally Wasowski, 1994)
Gardening with Nature in Texas (Karen M. Breneman, 2002)
Gardening with Prairie Plants: How to Create Beautiful Native Landscapes (Sally Wasowski, 2002)
How to Grow Native Plants of Texas and the Southwest (Jill Nokes, 2001)
Native Plants for Southwestern Landscapes (Judy Mielke, 1993)
Native Texas Gardens: maximum Buty Minimum Upkeep (Sally Wasowski, 2003)
Rare Plants of Texas: A Field Guide (Jackie M. Poole, 2007)
Remarkable Plants of Texas: Uncommon Accounts of Our Common Natives (Matt W. Turner, 2009)
Texas Wildflowers: A Field Guide (Campbell and Lynn Loughmiller, 2006)
Wild Orchids of Texas (Joe Liggio and Ann Orto Liggio, 1999)
Wildflowers Across Texas (Patricia Capertonn Parent, 2004)
Wildflowers of the Texas Hill Country (Marshall Enquist, 1987)

WILDLIFE GARDENING

Attracting Birds, Butterflies and Backyard Wildlife (David Mizejewski and Glee Barre, 2004)
Attracting Birds to Your Backyard: 536 Ways to Create a Haven for Your Favorite Brids (Susan A. Roth, 2003)
Backyard Birds of Texas (Bill Fennimore, 2008)
Birds of Texas (Fred J. Alsop, 2002)
Birds of Texas Field Guide (Stan Tekiela, 2004)
Butterfly Gardening for the South (Geyata Ajivsgi, 1991)
Butterflies of Houston and Southeast Texas (John Tveten and Gloria Tveten, 1996)
Finding Butterflies in Texas: A Guide to the Best Sites (Roland H. Wauer, 2006)
Texas Butterflies and Moths (James Kavanagh and Raymond Leng, 2007)
Texas Wildlife: An Introduction to Familiar Species (James Kavanagh, 2005)
Texas Wildscapes: Gardening for Wildlife (Noreen Damude and Kelly Conrad Bender, 1999)

PLANT/SEED SUPPLIERS

Antique Rose Emporium
10000 Hwy 50, Brenham, TX 77833
800-441-0002

David Austin Roses Ltd.
15059 Hwy. 64 West, Tyler, TX 75704
800-328-8893 www.davidaustinroses.com/american

Baker Creek Heirloom Seeds
2278 Baker Creek Rd. Mansfiled, MO 65704
417-924-8917 www.rareseeds.com

Bob Wells Nursery
17160 CR 4100, Lindale, TX 75771
903-882-3550 http://bobwellsnursery.com

Burpee
300 Park Avenue, Warminster, PA 18947
800-888-1447 www.burpee.com

The Cook's Garden
P.O. Box C5030, Warminster, PA 18974
800-457-9703 www.cooksgarden.com

Chamblee Rose Nursery
10926 U.S. Hwy. 69 North, Tyler, TX 75706-8742
903-882-5153 www.chambleeroses.com

Dixondale Farms
Box 129, Dept WP15, Carrizo Springs, TX 78834
877-367-1015 www.dixondalefarms.com

eGardeners Place
www.egardenersplace.com
800-335-4354

Fredericksburg Herb Farm
405 Whitney, Fredericksburg, TX 78624
830-997-8615 www.fredericksburgherbfarm.com

Harris Seeds
Box 24966, Rochester, NY 14624
800-544-7938 www.harrisseeds.com

Heirloom Seeds
287 E. Finley Drive, West Finley, PA 15377
www.heirloomseeds.com

High Mowing Seeds
76 Quarry Road, Wolcott, VT 05680
866-735-4454 www.highmowingseeds.com

Johnny's Selected Seeds
955 Benton Avenue, Winslow, ME 04901
877-564-6697 www.johnnyseeds.com

Kitazawa Seed Co.
201 4th Street, #206, Oakland, CA 94607
510-595-1188 www.kitazawaseed.com

Native American Seed
3791 N. US Hwy. 377
Junction, TX 76849 325-446-3600
www.seedsource.com/index.htm

Nichols Garden Nursery
1190 Old Salem Rd. NE, Albany, OR 97321
541-928-9280 www.nicholsgardennursery.com

The Nursery at Ty Ty
4723 U.S. Hwy. 82 W., Box 130, Ty Ty, GA 31795
888-758-2252 www.tytyga.com

Park Seed Co.
3507 Cokesbury Road, Hodges, SC 29653
800-854-3369 www.parkseed.com

The Pepper Gal
Box 23006, Ft. Lauderdale, FL 33307
954-537-5540 www.peppergal.com

Pinetree Garden Seeds
Box 300, New Gloucester, ME 04260
207-926-3400 www.superseeds.com

Potato Garden
12101 2135 Road, Austin, CO 81410
877-313-7783 www.potatogarden.com

Richters Herbs
357 Highway 47
Goodwood, Ontario, Canada L0C 1A0
905-640-6677 www.richters.com

Renee's Garden
6060 Graham Hill Road, Felton, CA 95018
888-880-7228 www.reneesgarden.com

Seeds of Change
Box 4908, Rancho Dominguez, CA 90220
888-762-7333 www.seedsofchange.com

Seed Savers Exchange
3094 North Winn Rd., Decorah, IA 52101
563-382-5990 www.seedsavers.org

Southern Exposure Seed
Box 460, Mineral, VA 23117
540-894-9480 www.southernexposure.com

Stokes Seeds
Box 548, Buffalo, NY 14240
800-396-9238 www.stokesseeds.co

Sustainable Seed Co
Box 38, Covelo, CA 95428
877-620-7333 www.sustainableseedco.com

Territorial Seeds
Box 158, Cottage Grove, OR 97424
800-626-0866 www.territorialseed.com

Tomato Growers Supply Co.
Box 60015, Fort Myers, FL 33906
888-478-7333 www.tomatogrowers.com

Totally Tomatoes
334 W. Stroud Street, Randolph, WI 53956
800-345-5977 www.totallytomato.com

Victory Seed Company
Box 192, Molalla, OR 97038
503-829-3126 www.victoryseeds.com

Wayside Gardens
1 Garden Lane, Hodges, SC 29653
800-845-1124 www.waysidegardens.com

Wildseed Farms
100 Legacy Drive, Fredericksburg, TX 78624
800-848-0078 www.wildseedfarms.com

Willhite Seed, Inc.
Box 23, Poolville, TX 76487-0023
800-828-1840 www.willhiteseed.com

Yucca Do Nursery
2597 County Road 133, Giddings, TX 78942
979-542-8811 www.yuccado.com

WHO ARE THE MASTER GARDENERS?

We are members of the local community who are willing to learn and help others and are able to communicate with diverse groups of people. What really sets Master Gardeners apart from other home gardeners is their special training in horticulture. Our mission is to be an educational, nonprofit, volunteer and service corporation which renders non-biased, sound horticultural information to the community. Master Gardeners work in partnership with the Texas Agrilife Extension and are the service arm of Extension Horticulture. Our objectives are accomplished through the volunteer efforts of Association Members.

Is the Master Gardener Program for Me?

To help you decide if you should apply to be a Master Gardener, ask yourself these questions:

- Do I want to learn more about the culture and maintenance of many types of plants?
- Am I eager to participate in a practical and intense training program?
- Do I look forward to sharing my knowledge with people in my community?
- Do I have enough time to attend training and to complete and continue the volunteer service?

If you answered yes to these questions, the Master Gardeners program could be for you.

Training

If accepted into the Master Gardeners program in your county, you will attend a Master Gardeners training course. Classes are taught by Texas A & M Agrilife Extension specialists, staff, and local experts.

The program offers a minimum of 50 hours of instruction that covers topics including lawn care; ornamental trees and shrubs; insect, disease, and weed management; soils and plant nutrition; vegetable gardening; home fruit production; garden flowers and water conservation.

Volunteer Commitment

In exchange for training, participants are obligated to volunteer time to their County Extension program. At least 50 hours of volunteer service within one year following the training is required to earn the title of "Texas Master Gardener."

The type of service done by Master Gardeners varies according to community needs, and the abilities and interests of the Master Gardeners. Current Travis County Master Gardeners Community Outreach projects include:

- Phone Support at the Travis County Agrilife Extension Office
- Plant Clinics at Nurseries and Zilker Botanical Garden
- Speakers' Bureau
- Docent Program at Zilker Botanical Garden
- School Garden Projects
- Web site with information for local gardeners: www.tcmastergardeners.org
- Publication of the Garden Guide for Austin & Vicinity
- Annual East Austin Garden Fair: A Passion for Plants
- Educational Garden Tour (every 18 months)
- Greenhouse projects including growing plants for Zilker Botanical Garden, Zilker Garden Festival and School Gardens
- Design, installation & maintainance of a Demonstration Garden at the Travis County Agrilife Extension Office

Master Gardeners are representatives of the Travis County Agrilife Extension. In all volunteer work related to the program, Master Gardeners follow the research-based recommendations of the Texas Agrilife Extension. The title "Texas Master Gardener" can be used by volunteers only when engaged in Agrilife Extension-sponsored activities.

Certification

Participants become certified Master Gardeners after they have completed the training course and fulfilled their volunteer commitment.

For additional information about the training programs and activities of the Travis County Master Gardeners, contact Daphne Richards, Travis County Agrilife Extension Agent-Horticulture, at 512-854-9600.

(Educational programs of the Texas Agrilife Service are open to all people without regard to race, color, religion, sex, national origin, age, disability, genetic information or veteran status. The Texas A&M University System, U.S. Department of Agriculture, and the County Commissioners Courts of Texas Cooperating)

INDEX